UnRetirement

A Career Guide for the Retired . . .
the Soon-to-Be Retired . . .
the Never-Want-to-Be Retired

Catherine Dorton Fyock
Anne Marrs Dorton

amacom

American Management Association

New York • Atlanta • Boston • Chicago • Kansas City • San Francisco • Washington, D.C.
Brussels • Mexico City • Tokyo • Toronto

This book is available at a special
discount when ordered in bulk quantities.
For information, contact Special Sales Department,
AMACOM, a division of American Management Association,
135 West 50th Street, New York, NY 10020.

This publication is designed to provide accurate and authoritative
information in regard to the subject matter covered. It is sold with
the understanding that the publisher is not engaged in rendering
legal, accounting, or other professional service. If legal advice or
other expert assistance is required, the services of a competent
professional person should be sought.

Library of Congress Cataloging-in-Publication Data

Fyock, Catherine D.
    UnRetirement / Catherine Dorton Fyock,
        Anne Marrs Dorton.
        p. cm.
    Includes bibliographical references and index.
    ISBN 0-8144-7865-4
    1. Aged—Employment—United States. 2. Retirees—Employment—
United States. 3. Age and employment—United States. I. Dorton,
Anne Marrs. II. Title.
    HD6280.F96 1994
    331.3'98'0973—dc20   93-49657
                                                              CIP

Printing number

10 9 8 7 6 5 4 3 2

To
Nancy and **Jack,**
with love

Contents

Anne's Introduction

These are exciting, challenging times for mature workers. I believe that there are more work opportunities for those of us who are fiftysomething, sixtysomething, seventysomething, *and older* than ever before in history. The sad thing to me is that so many wonderful, sought-after workers are sitting at home saying, "I'd love to work, but surely no one would hire me." Well, this book has been written to tell you that you *are* wanted and needed. It's also designed to tell you exactly how to go about marketing yourself and finding just the right spot—whether it be full-time, part-time, or any of the many other options that can be tailored just for you.

In order to establish my credibility in writing about all of this, let me tell you my story. Twenty years ago at the age of forty, I found myself a widow with three teenage children to support. I had worked as a secretary for four years when I was fresh out of school, but had left the workforce just before the birth of my first child and had not worked outside the home since. To say that I was terrified is an understatement, but I knew that I had to work—both for financial reasons and to save my sanity. To say that I received little encouragement is another understatement. In fact, my son, who was then fourteen years old, said to me, "Face it, Mom, you're never going to get a job. Nobody wants to hire someone who's forty years old." And from the depths of my despair I replied, "Well, you may be right, but at least I have to give it a try."

And give it a try I did. I searched the classified ads and found several temporary agencies that were advertising for secretaries. And—wonder of wonders—I was accepted, even after being tested and giving my true age! So the first lesson I learned was that miracles *do* happen, but first we have to ask for them.

I worked for the temporary agency for four years, and it was a wonderful transition back into the workforce. My skills were sharpened, my confidence grew, and I learned a great deal about the world of work. At the end of four years, I was ready for a full-time position. I had accepted a temporary position at a large local bank, and immediately felt at home there, so I was thrilled to accept their offer of a full-time job.

I worked first as a secretary and then as an administrative assistant at the bank. After seven years in three positions, a new position was created as supervisor of all the secretaries and administrative assistants in my division—and I was offered the job. This was a big step up for me. Suddenly I was an officer of the bank, and was supervising the workers who had been my peers. But I succeeded and received several nice promotions. I had come a long way from the terrified forty-year-old who believed that she might be too old to work!

But there was still something missing. I had never completed my undergraduate degree, and that bothered me. So, with the help of one of my young friends at the bank, I registered for my first night class—Introduction to Psychology—at the University of Louisville. The next semester I registered for two classes, and the next semester I took two more classes. By this time I was completely hooked on learning and made the decision to leave the bank and go back to school full-time in order to complete my degree in psychology.

Once again, there was not a great deal of enthusiasm or agreement among my family and friends about my new enterprise. A sample comment from one of my best friends went like this: "I respect your decision, and I respect your intelligence in making this decision. I just hope you won't regret it." The clear implication was that he feared I *would* regret it.

But I went ahead with my decision, and two years later received my degree in psychology—with honors, too! I was then fifty-six years old and wore my cap and gown and marched up onto that platform to receive my diploma with an enormous amount of satisfaction. I decided that I was on a roll and went on to receive my master's degree in counseling two years later.

So a quick arithmetic check shows that at graduation I was fifty-eight years old. Too old for a job? Up the proverbial creek? No! I received *three* job offers and chose to work as the vice president of my daughter's speaking and consulting firm, and she and I are collaborating on this book.

I firmly believe from my own experience and from what I have observed and learned and read—especially in my graduate studies in vocational counseling and in my work with a human resources consultant—that these are exciting, challenging times for older workers. I also know from my own experience how good it feels to work, to learn, to achieve—especially when a point is being proved. I proved my point: I was not too old to find a job, to be promoted, to earn two college degrees, or to find another job at the age of fifty-eight. And furthermore, *you can do it too*. This book is written to help you achieve your dreams in your own way. It can be done!

Cathy's Introduction

As a managment consultant, I have worked extensively in several areas of employment, particularly in the employment of older adults. I first became interested in the "graying of America" in the mid-1980s, when I was working for Kentucky Fried Chicken and facing some tremendous difficulties in recruiting and retaining the good employees we needed in our restaurants. We quickly discovered that targeting older adults for employment was an idea that worked brilliantly. This market segment, so often overlooked by other employers, was composed of mature, experienced workers who consistently proved to be an excellent choice for staffing our restaurants. When I left KFC to begin my consulting practice, I soon discovered that many other businesses were also studying the demographics and learning what an important resource older workers were going to be in "Workforce 2000"—the workforce of the twenty-first century.

In the fall of 1989 I wrote my first book, *America's Work Force Is Coming of Age: What Every Business Needs to Know to Recruit, Train, Manage, and Retain an Aging Work Force*. That first book, written from the employer's perspective, demonstrated for *organizations* the essential concepts involved in employing older adults. But as I traveled around the country, consulting with businesses and employment and training programs that offered placement services to older adults, I encountered many older individuals who were looking for an employment resource book written from *their* perspective—something that would help them resolve the numerous issues they faced. Many older adults told me that they wanted and needed to work yet couldn't seem to get back through the employment door because of the discriminatory practices still in existence. Many were unaware of the alternative workplace options now being considered by many employers. (Knowledge of such options as telecommuting and job sharing can be a powerful tool in negotiating with current employers about work scheduling to meet mutual needs.) Many told me they didn't know where to turn for help and assistance in resolving their employment problems. And many, as I learned from employment and training professionals who work with older adults, were hampered by self-defeating behaviors and attitudes that were creating unnecessary barriers to their return to work. Last but not least, many baby boomers told me that they were already concerned about aging and were beginning to examine options for working beyond their own "normal" retirement age.

When I discovered that there wasn't a sourcebook that addressed all these issues, I began to formulate the contents of this volume. The result is a comprehensive guide for older adults who want information on how to keep a job, how to get a job, how to explore and expand their work options, and how to resolve many of the other employment issues facing an aging America.

I know that when I reach "normal" retirement age, I want to have as many options available to me as possible. I intend to do my share to pave the road of expanding options for older "unretirees" because I believe that all of us should be able to realize our dreams, no matter what our age.

Chapter 1

Welcome to the
Unretirement Generation

Retirement is the ugliest word in the language.

—Ernest Hemingway

Aging is a relatively new phenomenon. Life expectancy in 1900 was only forty-seven. In contrast, a man turning sixty-five today can expect to live another fifteen years according to Census Bureau estimates. Life expectancy rates for women at age sixty-five are just under twenty years.[1]

Soon our life expectancy may reach eighty-five. With on-going advances in technology and the resulting increases in life expectancy, people are beginning to consider the implications for a society whose people are living longer, healthier lives. Older individuals are interested in remaining productive members of society long past "normal" retirement age.

In these exciting and changing times, older individuals are asking brand-new questions about what they will do with their longer lives and forging new patterns for living the balance of life in a way that is fulfilling and rewarding. Increasingly, older adults are beginning to ask: "What do I want to do with the rest of my life? Is it realistic to think that I should spend twenty years without working or being productive in some way?" Older individuals are no longer content to sit in a rocker or fill their days with golf, fishing, or gardening. As one older woman put it, "You can only repot so many pots and plant so many plants. Then it's time to do something more significant with your life."

Unretirement is the answer for these individuals. The fact that you are reading this book suggests that you are—or soon will be—one of them, that you are not satisfied with a life of idleness, that you want the challenges of work in some form, and that you are searching for ways to make this a reality. Chances are you are interested in finding challenging new life patterns that will permit you to realize your potential, contribute something to society, earn a reasonable living, and stimulate the mind and body. Unretirement is a method to achieve these goals.

Retirement: Traditional Patterns for Later Life

It wasn't until after World War II that retirement was common. The first Social Security benefits weren't paid until the early 1940s, and few employers provided pensions. People couldn't *afford* to retire.

After World War II, under a wartime wage freeze, unions negotiated pensions and other fringe benefits, thus making retirement feasible for the first time. The early retirement trend became a trickle in the 1960s and a torrent in the 1970s. Between 1960 and 1986, job rates for men ages fifty-five through sixty-four plunged to 67 percent from 87 percent.[2]

Retirement was accepted in our country after World War II, and normal retirement was established at age sixty-five. Then came the passage of the Age Discrimination in Employment Act (ADEA) in 1967, which prohibited discrimination on the basis of employment for those ages forty through seventy. ADEA was amended in 1984, and since that time, with the exception of those jobs in which age is a bona fide reason for disqualification of job candidates and retirement is mandatory (airline pilots, for example), there is no mandatory retirement age. It is now discriminatory for employers to disqualify or require retirement for employees solely on the basis of age.

After World War II, 90 percent of all American men between the ages of fifty-five and sixty-four either held jobs or were actively job hunting. Early retirement was shunned. A 1991 *New York Times* article quotes Gary Burtless, a Brookings

Institution senior fellow, as saying, "In 1950, if you were sixty years old and you were laid off, you tried just as hard to find a job as a forty-year-old." He commented that there were not a lot of pension plans, and early retirement, largely for this reason, was socially unacceptable. "Now there is no stigma to being a fifty-five-year-old healthy man, retired and living in Tempe, Arizona," he added.[3]

Yet while there is no stigma attached to being older and not working, many older adults are not content to sit idly by. Many find that they seek retirement, only to find themselves bored or depressed. Others discover that they want to follow a life's calling in some other vocational direction. And still others find that pensions, Social Security, and other income streams are inadequate to support their lifestyle. For these and many more reasons, unretirement seems to be an appealing alternative.

Unretirement: Nontraditional Roles for a New Order

The American Association of Retired Persons' (AARP) Worker Equity Department reports that since 1955, the number of older workers forty-five years of age and older has risen from 25 million to more than 33 million. Other reports show that the retirement trend is ebbing, as evidenced by a decreasing drop in labor force participation rates. Another indication is that the age at which men typically receive their first Social Security check has remained unchanged, at 63.7 years, since 1982. Previously, it had dropped fairly steadily since 1945.[4]

Other studies, such as that conducted by Louis Harris & Associates and commissioned by the Commonwealth Fund, a New York–based philanthropic organization, report an increasing interest among older individuals in seeking unretirement. The Commonwealth report of 1990 declares that more than 1.9 million older Americans ages fifty to sixty-four are ready and able to go back to work. (This is three times as many as the official government estimate of 630,000.) The survey reports that older adults are willing to accept jobs involving the following difficult employment conditions: seasonal work (83 percent); work done standing up (60 percent); work done alone (73 percent); work requiring a commute of more than thirty minutes (60 percent); and work done in evenings and weekends (54 percent).

In an article in the National Council on Aging's 1990 publication *Networks*, Thomas W. Moloney, senior vice president of the Commonwealth Fund, said, "This report should encourage business to look toward capable, committed older Americans to fill many [job] openings. They express a deeper commitment about returning to work and far more flexibility about the nature and conditions of the work they're looking for than any other surveys have suggested."

The Employment Perspective: A Puzzle With Mismatched Pieces

The emerging phenomenon of unretirement can be confusing in that it seems to be taking place in a context of mismatched puzzle pieces. For example, while there are many forces drawing older adults to the workplace and many forces encouraging businesses to employ older adults, there are still age discrimination cases, early-retirement incentives, and a seeming lack of strategies for effectively employing older adults.

Let's first examine, from the perspective of older individuals as well as from the perspective of the employers, some of the issues that are leading to the increased employment of older adults. Next we'll review the seeming paradoxes and try to make some sense of these puzzle pieces.

Your Side of the Unretirement Puzzle: Why Unretirement Is a Desirable Outcome

Older Adults Want to Work

In 1990 the Commonwealth Fund survey report estimated that nearly two million older adults were interested and ready to

work. According to John Russell, the president of Days Inn—
an organization that has worked extensively in the employment
of older adults—about five million older citizens nationwide
are looking for work.[5]

A 1988 study conducted by Caroline Bird through *Modern
Maturity* magazine asked workers over age fifty to complete a
questionnaire on options for second careers. Bird anticipated a
modest response of 2,000 or 3,000 readers. Instead, she was
deluged with over 36,000 responses.

In her questionnaire Bird asked about the reasons that
were drawing older adults to employment. Characteristically,
their responses, as described in her book *Second Careers*, were
extremely diverse, covering everything from the need to work
for financial reasons to the desire to get out of the house (or
away from a retired spouse!) to the challenge and enjoyment of
work itself.[6]

Here are some other reasons. Do any of these fit your
circumstances?

- To earn money
- To avoid welfare
- To pay off the mortgage
- To pay bills and meet expenses
- To pay for children's education
- To pay for or receive benefits to provide for an illness in
  the family
- To fill in the gaps in pension benefits
- To improve upon Social Security benefits
- To have money for extras
- To avoid a rapid physical decline, in the belief that
  retirement is dangerous
- To fight off the effects of aging, in the belief that working
  keeps you young
- To stay fit, in the belief that work is good for your
  physical and mental health
- To give structure and organization to your life
- To make a positive contribution at home, in the belief
  that work is good for family life

- To be with working family members or other people
- To get acquainted when new in town
- To continue business and professional contacts
- To be "a part of the world"
- To help individuals, groups, community, a cause, God, or the world at large
- To help a friend
- To help a family member run a business
- To further the interests of a disadvantaged group
- To pass on skills to others
- To fulfill a "need to be needed"
- To enjoy the experience of working
- To experience the joy of creating
- To fulfill a dream
- To experience the ideal job[7]

The Employer's Perspective: Why Employers Are Beginning to Value Unretirees

From the employers' standpoint, there are a number of reasons why unretirees are a valuable resource. Some of these reasons are described in the discussions that follow.

Labor Shortages: The Birth Dearth

Many employers today are facing labor shortages. This may seem incredible, given unemployment and slow economic times. But many employers are finding that the number of available new employees is waning because of something called the "birth dearth."

The "baby busters"—those individuals who are entering the workforce today—are far fewer in number than their counterparts in the baby boom generation twenty years ago. Baby boomers accounted for 72.5 million births in their generation (1945–1965); baby busters account for only 56.6 million births in theirs (1965–1985). Employers like those in the fast-food industry, who have traditionally relied on young workforce entrants, are already feeling the impact of the birth dearth on their workforce and beginning to recognize the need to turn to other labor market segments to meet their needs.

Older Adults' Special Skills

Exacerbating the effects of the birth dearth is the decrease in the number of *qualified* employees available to employers these days. With illiteracy on the rise, many young workforce entrants are ill prepared to handle the demands of high technology and the information age. Their youth and inexperience also leave many of them unqualified in such areas as communications, personal management, and group effectiveness. In addition, employers and job training specialists are finding that many young workers have problems with motivation, goal setting, creative thinking, and problem solving. As a result, some employers are beginning to look to older workers for the kind of skills they need to keep their businesses running.

Older Adults' Work Ethic and Outlook

Increasingly, employers are seeing the value of hiring people with a well-honed work ethic. Olsten Temporary Services, a national temporary help agency, has developed a recruitment initiative to target more-experienced individuals. Its program, titled Mature Advantage, is designed to attract older adults to temporary positions across the country. In a brochure called *Olsten Recognizes the Value of Maturity*, Olsten sings the praises of older adults, using such words as *dependable, responsible, efficient, productive,* and *enthusiastic* to describe them. In addition, Olsten states that it will not only bend over backward to make the temporary placement a success through training programs but will also make a contribution to a local nonprofit organization when an older adult enrolls.

Many employers find the outlook as well as the work ethic of younger workers quite different from those of unretirees. In a report entitled "The Age of Indifference," it was found that "young Americans, aged eighteen through thirty, know less and care less about news and public affairs than any other generation of Americans in the past fifty years."[8]

The Graying of the Workforce

The workforce is aging. Within the next twenty-five years, one in every four employees will be over the age of fifty-five. The average age of the American workforce has been creeping upward to its current average of nearly forty years of age. Employers are beginning to recognize the trend and are initiating strategies to better utilize this valuable resource.

The End of the "Tyranny of the Teenager"

For twenty years, fashion has slavishly followed the baby boom generation. And with the aging of this population segment, we are seeing the "decline of the tyranny of the teenager," according to Dr. Arthur Shostak, a fifty-five-year-old professor of sociology at Drexel University. Both a futurist and a specialist on aging, Shostak forecasts the shifting of the age pyramid and the refocus on older customers.[9]

Businesses today are beginning to understand the value of older customers. Sometimes referred to as *OPALS*—older persons with active lifestyles—this newly important customer segment has buying power and clout.

But older adults want to purchase products and services to meet *their* needs, not the needs of a twenty-five-year-old. Consider the story of Morton Yulish, age fifty-one. When he went shopping for a new car, he found that all the salespeople were delivering sales pitches geared to younger buyers. They kept emphasizing the power of the radio and the engine when what he was looking for was a car with safety and integrity. Yulish, who is a consultant focusing on the mature market, says that businesses can either "benefit from it or be a victim of it."[10]

Silver and Gold, a publication developed in the St. Cloud, Minnesota, community, is strictly for businesses serving the unique needs of older adults. The publication offers services from senior banking to pharmacy discounts to apartments with one living level and no steps. Many businesses are beginning to see that an understanding of older adults and what they want and need will mean their survival in the years to come.

And they are also learning that those who best understand the needs of older customers are older workers.

The Paradox: Why Unretirement Is Still in Its Infancy

Days Inn has discovered that attracting unretirees is good business. Yet ironically, other employers have not caught on to the value of hiring experience, says Days Inn president John Russell. "For all our talking about it, older people are still the best-kept secret when it comes to hiring loyal, steady and capable employees."[11]

The SHRM/AARP Study

The Society for Human Resource Management and AARP conducted a survey of more than 1,000 human resources professionals, and discovered that unretirees are overwhelmingly seen as valuable employees. According to 87 percent of the respondents, the two most valuable assets of older workers are experience and skill—qualities that are often lacking in new entrants to the workforce. Unretirees' additional assets include: less absenteeism (65 percent), greater motivation (62 percent), and excellent skills in mentoring younger workers (60 percent). In addition, 67 percent of human resources professionals valued older workers' flexibility—specifically, their willingness to work as part-time or temporary employees.

Paradoxically, the same human resources professionals who saw such positive benefits in older adults also failed to provide programs to encourage unretirees to stay on the job. Fewer than three out of ten employers maintain specific programs to retain unretirees.

The Rise in Age Discrimination Claims

Another paradox is the rise in age discrimination claims. In 1981, the Equal Employment Opportunity Commission (EEOC) reported that 12,710 charges of age discrimination had been filed. In 1987, the number of charges filed increased to 24,963.

Claims jumped 20 percent in 1991 to 28,333. AARP stated that it responded to 105,000 requests for information about age discrimination in 1991, a 155 percent increase from a year earlier.

Why—in the face of existing labor shortages and the lack of qualified employees, older workers' proven advantages in terms of skills and values, and their willingness to work part-time or on a temporary basis—does there continue to be a rise in age discrimination charges? This intriguing issue will be discussed in Chapter 8.

The Double-Edged Sword of Fast-Food Employment

Another dilemma faced by many older adults seeking employment is posed by the fact that a small group of employers— primarily quick-service restaurants—*have* shown a decided interest in hiring older workers. "It seemed that only the fast-food employers were interested in us," stated one frustrated older adult seeking professional employment at a community job fair. "Entry-level jobs are fine for those who want them, but I'm looking for a living wage," said another job seeker in need of the salary and benefits often lacking in job offerings to unretirees.

When this book was being written, one cynical friend commented, "Why are you writing a book on unretirement when the only ones who want to hire older adults are those who want to exploit them?" While fast-food employers are indeed interested in hiring older adults, there is a growing perception that these service employers frequently take advantage of older adults at a time when other employers are not interested.

Early-Out Programs

Many employers these days seem determined to implement "early-out" programs designed to downsize, or "rightsize" their organization during a restructuring process. While this strategy has proved to be successful for many employers who want to reduce their workforce, it is often a strategy that results in forcing out older adults, with the result that employers are not benefiting from the wealth of experience in this work group.

The American Dream: Retirement

"Early retirement became a kind of status symbol," says Harold Sheppard, gerontology professor at the University of South Florida. "It was an outward sign of success, showing you didn't have to work if you didn't want to."[12] But this trend is reversing. In 1988, 68.8 percent of men age sixty and over remained in the workforce; since then, 70.7 percent of men sixty and over have remained in the workforce.

Putting the Pieces of the Puzzle Together

As the foregoing discussions make clear, the employment picture for older adults is currently filled with contradictions. Nonetheless, we are beginning to see the emergence of forces that will help to bring together unretirees like you who want to work and employers who know your value and want to hire you. Outlined here are some of these developments and the ways you can follow up on them. All will be covered in more detail in later chapters of the book.

Finding Work Options That Meet Your Needs

All too frequently you are offered two options in the workforce—work full-time or retire—when, in reality, you may want some option in the middle. Part-time, phased retirement options, job-sharing, temporary assignments, and other work options are often very appealing if you want to work fewer hours for reasons of health and stamina, a desire to more effectively balance home and work responsibilities, a wish to spend more time with grandchildren, or an interest in traveling or meeting other needs.

More frequently, employers are offering alternative work

options and staffing programs to an entire workforce that is trying to balance work and home responsibilities and values flexibility. You may find that these same alternatives meet *your* need to work while fulfilling your other life responsibilities and wishes.

Finding Employers Who Recognize Your Value

Why is it so difficult to identify the employers who want to find unretirees like you who want to work? What we are discovering is that today's job market is often a *hidden* job market. Just a few years ago, if you were searching for a job, you merely had to go to the largest employer in your community to find someone looking for good employees. Today, the growth in jobs is coming from small and midsize employers, not mega-employers. These small and midsize companies often have a low profile and, while they are growing, are often unknown to you. It is often these employers who are the most ready and willing to value maturity, experience, and judgment over youth.

Further, there are many employers who recognize the value of older adults, but who are not yet knowledgeable about how to effectively reach this group. Counselors and job-search professionals can provide valuable assistance to you when you do not have any way of identifying these employers.

Finding Services to Assist You

You may need assistance in identifying the employers who will welcome you and in finding specific job-search information that will assist you in the process of résumé preparation, job-search strategies, dealing with age discrimination, and other issues.

A number of government-funded programs help older adults find these services. If you are interested in identifying professionals to assist in your job search, you can contact the Private Industry Council, your state unit on aging, or any number of national older worker programs operated through funding provided by the Older Americans Act. Refer to the Appendix for specific resource information.

Fighting Back as Part of the Unretirement Generation

Age discrimination charges are on the rise. The good news for you is that unretirees who feel that their jobs have been compromised because of their age are fighting back, and employers are taking notice.

Employers are becoming more aware of this issue, and are more carefully examining old policies that may adversely affect their older employees. Editorial articles on age discrimination, such as "Age Discrimination Cannot Continue" in the October 1992 edition of *HRMagazine*, focus on businesses' need to review their employment practices. As the author, John R. Hundley, states, "Enlightened management will realize that age discrimination in employment is a reemerging issue. They will review their employment policies and practices to ensure they are truly hiring the best candidates without regard to age."

Riding on the Success of Other Unretirees

Success breeds success, and there are plenty of success stories about how employers have benefited from the employment of older workers. Doug Mangum, vice president and manager of a Texas Commerce Bank branch, tells of hiring a sixty-year-old woman who is a former bank vice president. She wanted part-time work and a less stressful job, and finds her work as a lobby teller a very satisfying one that meets her needs. It also meets the bank's needs; her manager reports that her work is excellent.[13]

Georgene Richaud, director of human resources for the Stouffer Austin Hotel, actively recruits unretirees even when they have a seemingly unrelated work background. She finds that older adults generally make excellent employees because of their life experience and level of judgment.[14]

The testimony of these and other employers is providing

food for thought for other businesses that had not considered focusing employment efforts on older adults.

What Do Employers Really Want and What Do You Have to Offer?

What is it that employers are really looking for in their employees? Nearly every business today subscribes to the following priorities:

- *Improved productivity.* Employers need to produce their goods or services in an efficient manner in order to realize the greatest profits. As an older adult, you can meet these needs by demonstrating that you can work productively, with fewer mistakes, and with higher quality.
- *Reduced absenteeism and tardiness.* For every day that an employee is out sick or late to work, the employer loses money. As an unretiree, you are likely to have a better attendance record and a lower incidence of tardiness, and can help the employer's bottom line in this regard.
- *Employees with the right skills mix.* In light of the birth dearth and fewer job candidates with the right abilities, skills, and knowledge, you can offer employers what they are looking for.
- *Employee loyalty.* When employees are loyal, turnover decreases and retention rates improve, helping employers reduce the costs of turnover: selection costs, training costs, costs associated with a new inexperienced employee, etc. Because you, as an unretiree, tend to stay on the job longer than a younger counterpart, you can offer a company a greater return on its employee dollar.
- *Increased employee morale.* When employees are satisfied on the job, they tend to be more productive and more loyal, contributing to the employer's bottom line. If you work because you want to work, not because you have to, you will help your company meet its needs in this department.

- *A quality product or service to offer the customer*. Because you, as an unretiree, tend to value service and quality, it is to the employer's advantage to have you on the team.

Identifying and Overcoming Barriers to Your Unretirement

Given the employers' needs and your abilities to meet those needs, there are barriers you may need to overcome in your quest toward unretirement.

- *Negative perceptions about unretirees*. As we will discuss in Chapter 2, there are numerous negative misconceptions about the abilities, motivations, and needs of unretirees. In addition, discrimination still remains a barrier to the employment of older adults. In fact, in the survey conducted by Caroline Bird, 42 percent of the older workers responding indicated that they faced some sort of discrimination on the job.[15] Many younger bosses feel threatened by having older employees reporting directly to them.
- *Work schedules that may not meet your needs*. While flexible scheduling arrangements are growing in popularity, they are still not the norm in today's workplace. Caroline Bird's survey showed that 8 percent of those responding indicated that scheduling imposed a barrier to employment.
- *Salaries that may not meet your needs*. Twenty-five percent of the respondents in Bird's survey indicated that pay was a problem in employment.
- *Being part of the "sandwich" generation*. This is the phenomenon of having children/grandchildren to care for, as well as parents/grandparents who need care. Many of today's employees are caught in the middle and find that balancing work and family care responsibilities is extremely difficult.

Other issues that may create obstacles include:

* Your health and the health of others
* Social Security earnings limitation
* Family objections to your working
* Problems in balancing work and leisure

Finally, there is another barrier to the employment of older adults that is so pervasive it merits an entire section of its own. This barrier, mostly self-imposed, is the negative view of their abilities and prospects held by many older adults themselves. This subject will be discussed in detail in Chapter 10.

Employers Who Are Putting Experience Back to Work

Where can you find employers who value experience, maturity, and judgment? Consider these employers with a record of hiring unretirees or providing a workplace conducive to the needs of their older employees:

GRUMMAN AEROSPACE COMPANY, in Bethpage, New York, has a vested interest in retaining its experienced workers because it is difficult and costly to gain security clearance for new employees.

WALT DISNEY WORLD COMPANY, in Lake Buena Vista, Florida, employs unretirees in about 9 percent of its positions throughout the organization.

THE TRAVELERS CORPORATION, in Hartford, Connecticut, hires unretirees for its job bank—a pool of workers who staff temporary assignments throughout its operations.

CONTROL DATA CORPORATION, in Minneapolis, has initiated a new business advisers division composed of its retired professionals. Employees from this division are hired by outside firms as independent consultants.

HARDEE'S FOOD SYSTEMS, INC., headquartered in Rocky Mount, North Carolina, KENTUCKY FRIED CHICKEN, based in Louisville, Kentucky, and other quick-service restaurants have recognized the value of unretirees in meeting their staffing needs for dependable, mature employees.

BUILDERS EMPORIUM, headquartered in Irvine, California, has discovered that unretirees understand customer service issues better than younger workers because they themselves come from a do-it-yourself generation.

JOSEPH HORN DEPARTMENT STORE, in Pittsburgh, prefers older workers; 32 percent of its hourly positions are staffed by unretirees.

HONEYWELL CORPORATION, in Minneapolis, goes the extra mile in providing a workplace that is unretiree-friendly. It accomplishes this aim through an advisory committee called the Older Workers League (OWL) composed of all company workers over the age of fifty.

WAL-MART STORES, INC., based in Arkansas, employs unretirees because Wal-Mart recognizes the demographic trends, and wants its workforce to match the demographics of its customer base.[16]

Aging, retirement, and unretirement: These are the challenges and the opportunities for today's older adults—you. Is retirement the true American dream, or is the *real* dream for some other alternative that offers a means to be active, to earn income, to remain challenged, to be with other people, and to be stimulated by the opportunities of work, on terms to be decided by the individual with experience, maturity, and judgment?

There are as many forces compelling older adults to seek unretirement options as there are forces making the employment of older adults attractive for employers. Yet there are still many puzzling issues, including the fact that, side by side with employers' favorable perceptions of older workers, there are few policies and practices to support their employment, increasing charges of age discrimination, and no end in sight to early retirement policies.

Your challenge in seeking unretirement options will be to

capitalize on the trends that are beginning to take place: increased flexibility for older adults (and other workers, too); more employment services tailored to the needs of older job seekers; increasing numbers of success stories regarding the employment of older adults; and the restructuring of retirement and unretirement policies by employers.

You, as a member of today's unretirement generation, are truly a pioneer setting out to stake new claims, settle new territory, and blaze new trails into the world of work for older Americans today and tomorrow.

Notes

1. Robert Lewis, "Early Out—All at Once, the Party's Over," *AARP Bulletin*, June 1992.
2. Ibid.
3. Louis Uchitelle, "Why Older Men Keep on Working," *New York Times*, April 23, 1991.
4. Lewis, "Early Out."
5. Ernest Holsendolph, "Older Workers Helped to Jobs in Tough Market," *Atlanta Journal/Atlanta Constitution*, May 28, 1993.
6. Caroline Bird, *Second Careers* (New York: Little, Brown and Co., 1992).
7. Ibid.
8. Christine D. Keen, *HRNews*, August 1990.
9. Joanna Biggar, "Future May Hold Special Roles for Senior Citizens," *Saginaw News*, July 14, 1991.
10. Neill A. Borowski, "Gray Power," *Chicago Tribune*, June 2, 1991.
11. Holsendolph, "Older Workers Helped."
12. Lewis, "Early Out."
13. Al Ebbers, "It's Back to Work They Go," *Human Resource Executive*, August 1990.
14. Ibid.
15. Bird, *Second Careers*.
16. Catherine D. Fyock, *America's Work Force Is Coming of Age: What Every Business Needs to Know to Recruit, Train, Manage, and Retain an Aging Work Force* (Lexington, Mass.: Lexington/Macmillan, 1990).

Chapter 2

Overcoming Employers' Misconceptions About Unretirees

Career advancement is much like marketing; your objective is to position yourself as the ideal solution to an organizational need.

—J. Paul Costello, President, Costello Erdlen & Company

Have you had the experience of being turned down for a job because of your age? Have you felt yourself being labeled "too old to work"? Have you felt that it was pointless to send out another résumé because of the youth-oriented thinking of many of today's employers? You are not alone.

Many unretirees attempting to keep jobs or, worse yet, to find employment in today's job market find themselves facing ageism, age discrimination, and negative stereotypical thinking about older workers. Employers do have fears about older adults and believe that they will be a detriment to the organization.

It's important for you to understand just what these misconceptions are, to differentiate between the myths and the realities by understanding the facts, and to develop some specific strategies for either keeping your job or finding an unretirement option that meets your needs.

We have identified fifteen myths about older workers. We'll discuss each of these in terms of employers' real beliefs and then look at the facts about each myth and uncover the realities. In each case, we'll provide action steps for countering these points of resistance when dealing with employers.[1]

Myth 1: Older Adults Are Not Interested in Working

Many employers believe that those who can afford retirement should enjoy their retirement and not seek unretirement. Since retirement has been the American dream, they argue, why employ older adults who'll only quit as soon as they can or whenever they want?

Reality: Many Older Adults Are Interested in Working

As we've already outlined in Chapter 1, there are numerous reasons why older adults seek unretirement. The love of a challenge, the need to be intellectually engaged, the desire to be with other people, the need to escape idleness, the joy of feeling productive and helping others—all can be powerful motivations for working, even when, in strictly financial terms, one can afford to retire.

Many older adult are also interested in working if they can find work that enables them to juggle other priorities: family, travel, outside interests and hobbies, and volunteer and leisure activities. For these individuals, alternative work schedules—such as telecommuting, job-sharing, consulting, and flextime—are an excellent solution.

Strategies for Keeping Your Job

- Communicate your interest in remaining an active contributor on the job.
- Let others know of your desire to work an alternative work schedule.

Strategies for Finding a Job

- Talk with prospective employers about work options, especially if you want to work temporary or part-time

assignments. Employers often find it difficult to fill this
type of position with qualified, motivated employees.
* Communicate your varied reasons for working during
  the interview process. Let interviewers know that you
  are motivated by more than money, but don't let an
  interviewer compromise your salary or benefits as a
  result.

Myth 2: Unretirees Are Slow, Unproductive Workers

Many employers' image of older people is of grandmotherly or
grandfatherly figures sitting in rocking chairs knitting or whit-
tling. Some employers cannot imagine older adults involved in
energetic and physically demanding tasks such as heavy lifting
and standing for long periods of time. Others are unable to
think of older adults in fast-paced work environments where
everyone works with a sense of urgency. As common as it is to
see older adults working in fast-food environments these days,
there are still many managers who are reluctant to hire older
adults for fear that they cannot "keep up."

Reality: Unretirees Are Productive Workers

Research has shown that age is a poor predictor of mental and
physical abilities and that, when a correlation does exist, it
shows that performance tends to *improve* with age! Other
studies have shown that older adults tend to participate in
many unpaid productive activities.

Older adults are often more deliberate in their activities,
but tend to perform them with fewer errors, thus making theirs
a more productive performance. Further, with fewer on-the-
job accidents, older adults are really more productive than their
younger counterparts.

Strategies for Keeping Your Job

* Be aware of productivity measures in your organization.
  Check to see how you compare. Note other contributing

factors to productivity in addition to work output, such as quality of work performed, amount of rework needed, waste, and accidents.

* Ask for performance reviews on a regular basis. See if there are ways to strengthen your on-the-job performance.

Strategies for Finding a Job

* Provide information on your background, whether on your résumé or in the interview, in terms of your achievements. Show prospective employers that you have made valuable contributions in the past.
* Demonstrate by examples and specific details how you remain active in your chosen field. Are you still an active member of your professional association? Do you speak and write on topics in your field? Do you read new literature on your topic?
* Show that you are physically active and able to handle the physical demands of the job. Stress your good health. Talk about your physical activities. (Do you walk two miles every day, for example?)

Myth 3: Older Adults Don't Want to Work Because of Their Social Security Benefits

Many employers make the assumption that Social Security puts older adults on easy street and wonder why anyone eligible for the benefits would want to work and jeopardize these benefits. Some may even believe that all Social Security benefits are eliminated once someone works.

Reality: Many Older Adults Are Not Yet Eligible for Social Security Benefits, or Find That Working Offsets Any Loss in Social Security Benefits

First of all, many older adults are not yet eligible for Social Security benefits. These younger older workers are not yet eligible for these and other pension benefits, so often have a very real need to work.

Second, older adults over age seventy can work all they want and not jeopardize their Social Security benefits at all.

Finally, many older adults recognize that the benefits of working outweigh any loss of Social Security they may experience. Some choose to delay their benefits. Others realize that since benefits are not jeopardized in a dollar-for-dollar fashion, most people who work can earn more money than if they didn't work at all.

Strategies for Keeping Your Job

- Communicate with your employers about your plans for unretirement. Let them know about your motivations for working.
- Before you quit your job to earn Social Security benefits, carefully explore the amount of benefits you will receive, noting how much you can earn before benefits are jeopardized and how many benefit dollars you will lose by earning an additional dollar.

Strategies for Finding a Job

- As in the notation above, explore what you wish to earn before applying for a job. Determine what benefits you are eligible for and what additional earnings will contribute to your bottom line.
- Don't let prospective employers make assumptions about your reliance on Social Security benefits. Clearly communicate your needs to them.

Myth 4: Unretirees Don't Need or Want to Work

Some employers believe that all older adults have generous pension incomes, have no major expenses, are comfortably retired, and just want to sit in the sun all day. (Perhaps because this is their own dream for the future!) They find it hard to believe that someone with a comfortable pension would be interested in working instead of golfing or fishing.

Reality: Many Unretirees Do Need or Want to Work

Many older adults who once believed that their pensions or Social Security benefits would more than provide for their later years are finding they were sadly mistaken. Increasing living costs, decreasing pension benefits and retiree health insurance, illness, the need to provide for other family members, rising home repair costs, and many other factors can make a paycheck necessary.

As one older woman told us, she was receiving pensions from several of her past jobs as well as getting Social Security, yet she found she couldn't do everything she wanted without supplementing her income with some paid work. As she points out, "If it isn't the leaking roof, it's another car repair or a new washer or dryer . . . it's always something." She's discovered that part-time and temporary work assignments fit the bill, enabling her to pay for any extra things she needs or wants and still have enough mney to support herself day to day.

Strategies for Keeping Your Job

- Let employers know of your interest in remaining active on the job. Tell them that you intend to work past "normal" retirement if that is your intention.
- Communicate your interest in an alternative work arrangement, such as part-time, temporary, job-sharing, or other flexible schedule. (See Chapter 3 for more information on unretirement options.)

Strategies for Finding a Job

- Tell prospective employers of your need to work. Employers like to hire people when they understand their motivation to work. And when they see that the individual both wants and needs to work, they believe that individual will remain with the organization longer, thus decreasing their cost relative to turnover.

- Explain when your motivations for work are nonfinan-
cial. Stress the importance of the intrinsic rewards you
receive from work, such as the satisfaction you get from
doing a good job, making a contribution, working with
fellow employees and customers, and helping others.

Myth 5: Unretirees Are Inflexible and Resistant to Change

Many employers believe that people get more rigid and set in
their ways as they age. They think that older people will be
cranky and uncooperative and say things like, "I tried that
before and it didn't work," or "That idea will never fly."

*Reality: Flexibility and Willingness to Change Is a Personality
Trait That Remains Fixed Throughout a Person's Lifetime*

Since openness to change and adaptability are personality
traits, it is likely that someone who is inflexible as an older
person was also inflexible as a young person. Similarly, those
who are adaptable and flexible as young people usually remain
adaptable and flexible as older people.

Strategies for Keeping Your Job

- Demonstrate your willingness to change. When the organization introduces a new program or procedure, look
for ways to actively support that change.
- Should you perceive problems in dealing with an organizational change, express your criticisms in a positive,
constructive manner.

Strategies for Finding a Job

- Show prospective employers that you are an individual
who responds well to change. Share specific examples
of how you have been able to adapt to a recent change.
- Avoid phrases like, "I did that before and it didn't
work."

Myth 6: Unretirees Have No Interest in Advancing

Employers believe that older workers are just looking for a job to pass the time. Many believe that older workers want humdrum, nonchallenging work. Others believe that all older workers are only looking for work as a means to be with other people or avoid boredom. Such employers fail to realize that many older adults are seeking work as a way of earning their livelihood. They also find it hard to understand that some older adults want challenging work to stimulate their minds, and that they want the pay and financial rewards that accompany that work.

Reality: Many Unretirees Want to Advance and to Find Challenges in Their Work

There are countless stories about older adults who have achieved greatness later in life. Further, no one wants to feel that there are limits placed on his or her ability or potential to perform. And while it is true that some older adults are working for reasons other than the need for challenge and responsibility, this is hardly the case for all members of the group.

Strategies for Keeping Your Job

- Communicate to your boss your expectations for growth and development. Let your boss know if you have career aspirations within the organization.
- Look for the challenges in your work. Many jobs today can expand to fit the motivations and capabilities of the individuals who fill them. Look for opportunities for job enlargement, and the corresponding financial rewards.
- Find out what is required to move up to the next rung on the career ladder. Begin now to prepare to meet those requirements.

Strategies for Finding a Job

- Let interviewers know that you are still learning and growing in your professional development. Let them

know of your willingness to do what it takes to get ahead.
 • Continue with your career development and communicate your activities to your prospective employer.

Myth 7: Unretirees Won't Remain With the Company for Very Long

Employers are afraid of employee turnover; turnover costs them big bucks. Turnover dollars really begin to add up when you compute the cost of hiring new people, training them on the new job, bringing them up to speed, and correcting the errors they're likely to make at the beginning. All these factors have a negative impact on productivity.

Many employers believe that older adults won't be on the job for long. They think everyone wants to leave the job market as soon as possible, and they question the motives of older adults who could retire instead of unretire.

Reality: Unretirees Remain on the Job Longer Than Their Younger Counterparts

Studies consistently show that older workers are more likely to remain on the job than their younger counterparts. In fact, *first careerists*—those employed in their first job—generally plan to leave their first employer unless they find some compelling reason to remain on the job. Older adults are less transient, more loyal, and, while they theoretically have fewer years to offer their employers, tend to remain on the job longer. Some companies, such as Western Savings and Loan of Arizona and First Savings of San Diego, have developed strategies to recruit older workers precisely because of their higher retention rates.

Strategies for Keeping Your Job

 • Let your employer know that you intend to work as long as you are able. Do this by talking with your supervisor and sharing your plans.
 • Demonstrate your continued interest in employment by

continuing to invest in your professional development
and training. Attend company-sponsored educational
programs. Take a college or vocational education course.
Enroll in a seminar or workshop.

* Simply outlast your younger counterparts! Nothing
  speaks louder than your loyalty and commitment to your
  employer.

Strategies for Finding a Job

* Let prospective employers know that you are planning
  to make a long-term commitment to their ogranization.
  Discuss your interest in remaining active.
* Show an interest in company-sponsored training and
  development programs. Demonstrate your willingness
  to participate in these programs.
* Ask about the short-term and long-term goals of the
  organization. Share information about how you might
  contribute to the achievement of these goals over time.

Myth 8: Unretirees Are Often Absent From Work Because of Illness

Some people think of older adults as they would a frail, sick
relative. They fail to see older adults as healthy, competent,
energetic, active people, and therefore fear that they will have
high absenteeism and tardiness rates.

Reality: Unretirees Tend to Have Less Incidence of Absenteeism and Tardiness Than Their Younger Counterparts

Study after study confirms that older workers' absenteeism
and tardiness rates are lower than those of their younger
counterparts. Statistics compiled by companies like Polaroid
and Banker's Life show that older employees have a far greater
incidence of perfect attendance than any other group in the
workforce.

Furthermore, few companies have actually reported problems with older adults arriving late to work. If there tends to

be a problem, it is with older workers arriving too early! We continue to hear stories about older adults who are the only ones to arrive during blizzards or power outages. And there's at least one story about an older worker who has been late for her 4:00 A.M. shift only once—the first day of daylight savings time, when she forgot to set her clock forward.

Strategies for Keeping Your Job

- It may sound obvious, but arrive on time, and don't miss work! Call as far in advance as possible when you know you will be unable to work due to illness, weather, or for some other reason.
- Let your employer know that you understand the importance of being at work on time every day.

Strategies for Finding a Job

- Arrive promptly for interviews (but not more than five or ten minutes early—this can send a signal that you don't value time, or that you don't have a sense of urgency).
- Talk about your record for attendance and punctuality with your previous employers, or in nonpaid work assignments.

Myth 9: Unretirees Incur Higher Insurance Costs

Many employers with an eye on the bottom line are concerned about the higher insurance costs they may incur when hiring older workers. And in some cases, their fears are justified; insurance costs for older workers *may* be higher.

Reality: Insurance Costs Are Not Necessarily Higher When Unretirees Are Employed.

Some studies do in fact show higher insurance costs for older adults, yet other studies have concluded that costs aren't necessarily higher. A study by Yankelovich, Skelly, and White,

Inc., reported that many employers actually feel that their insurance costs were higher for employees during their child-bearing years than for older adults. This finding was especially true of younger older adults (those in their mid-fifties).[2]

Strategies for Keeping Your Job

◆ Remain active and take proactive steps to ensure a healthy lifestyle.

Strategies for Finding a Job

◆ Share information with prospective employers that will demonstrate your commitment to a healthy, active life-style.

Myth 10: Unretirees Are Expensive to Train

Studies have demonstrated that it can take older employees as much as twice as long to learn new tasks. For employers considering the training or retraining of their employees, this added training time can mean real dollars subtracted from the bottom line.

"You can't teach an old dog new tricks" is still an idea held by many. Also, even when there is not the concern about older workers' ability to learn, there is still the recognition that many older adults have not had as much exposure to high technology as the younger generation has and may find it more difficult to learn to use computers, electronic cash registers, high-tech office equipment, and the like.

Reality: The Training Investment for Employers Is Quickly Repaid by Unretirees

The fact is that since older workers tend to stay on the job longer, the increased time invested in their training (in those instances when a longer training time *is* needed) is quickly repaid. It is also repaid by older adults' ability to retain infor-mation longer and perform a job with fewer mistakes

While it may be true that you can't teach an old *dog* new tricks, that adage certainly doesn't hold true for human beings. Older adults can indeed learn new technology with the proper instruction.

In some occupations, older adults may actually be able to learn the job more quickly (especially if it is similar to work they've done in the past) because older adults have a greater fund of experience to draw upon.

Strategies for Keeping Your Job

* Keep up with your professional development. Never pass up an opportunity to keep learning and growing on the job, or you may find yourself unprepared for future changes in your organization.
* Develop a can-do attitude when it comes to learning new tasks or procedures.
* Should you need extra assistance in learning new technology in your organization, seek it out. Get a tutor. Attend an outside class. Do what it takes to keep up.

Strategies for Finding a Job

* Tell prospective employers about any current education and training you're engaged in. On your résumé, include any recent degrees you've earned, any workshops you've attended, and any other recent learning experiences that show you *can* learn new tricks.
* Discuss your interest in learning new concepts, procedures, and ideas. Let employers know that you are not afraid to learn and grow professionally.

Myth 11: Unretirees Are More Accident-Prone

Some employers have nightmarish visions of older workers breaking a hip or receiving some other major injury while on the job. They're concerned about potential increases in workers compensation costs—not to mention the guilt they'd feel for having made such an injury possible. Like overprotective parents, they feel that they shouldn't put older workers in a position where they might be hurt.

Reality: Unretirees Have Fewer On-the-Job Accidents Than Their Younger Counterparts

In study after study, unretirees have proved that they work with care and concern and understand the importance of safety. They are deliberate and don't make the same mistakes as their younger, less thoughtful counterparts. The fact is that older workers are safe, conscientious workers.

Strategies for Keeping Your Job

* Stay alert to safety hazards. Don't become careless, especially when you get familiar with a job.

Strategies for Finding a Job

* Stress your accident-free work record. Talk about the importance of safety on the job.

Myth 12: Unretirees Are Not as Adept Intellectually

Employers are afraid that older employees won't be as sharp mentally as their younger counterparts. They fear that the memories of older employees are fading and they won't be able to handle the mental challenges of the job.

Reality: Unretirees Are as Mentally Agile as Their Younger Counterparts

Most studies indicate that intellectual functioning remains intact until we are in our seventies and, for many individuals, beyond this age. Further, since older adults tend to be more deliberate in their activities, they usually perform their work with fewer mistakes. Though they may take longer to train, they usually retain information longer

Strategies for Keeping Your Job

- Make a continued commitment to staying current on the job.
- Develop a system to keep yourself organized at the office and at home. Present an image of being "together."

Strategies for Finding a Job

- Use the interviewer's name in the interview. Make notes of details to remember.
- Provide examples of difficult challenges you have faced recently in your work. Demonstrate your ability to solve problems and to follow a logical sequence in decision making.

Myth 13: Unretirees Are Difficult to Work With

There are a number of terms that connote the negative traits associated with older persons. "Crotchety," "battle-ax," "nag," "buzzard," "coot" (often prefaced by the word *old*) are just some of the many terms that relay the notion that older adults are difficult human beings. Supervisors don't want to hire trouble, and they want to avoid any chance of bringing a problem employee onto their work site.

Reality: Because of Their Life Experience, Many Unretirees Have Enhanced Interpersonal Skills and Abilities

The reality is that most older adults, with a lifetime of experience behind them, have very well-developed interpersonal skills. Further, since many older adults place a high value on courtesy, tact, and diplomacy, they tend to work easily with co-workers and customers.

In fact, many employers who have begun hiring older workers for the first time are discovering that older adults provide a tremendous stabilizing force within a younger workforce. Mentoring relationships are not uncommon, with younger employees seeking the counsel and wisdom of older co-workers in a nonthreatening relationship.

Strategies for Keeping Your Job

- Develop a reputation for being "easy to get along with" in the organization.
- Play the role of facilitator when appropriate.
- Mentor or support the career development of younger co-workers or subordinates.

Strategies for Finding a Job

- Stress your ability to work with your co-workers, supervisors, and customers in past work experiences. Share examples, when practical, that demonstrate your ability to work as a part of a team. (This can be especially crucial in view of the fact that many companies are moving toward self-directed work teams.)
- Be pleasant in interviews. Don't make excessive demands during the hiring process. Prove that you are a reasonable business person.

Myth 14: Older Workers Are Viewed Negatively by Customers

Some employers believe that their youthful customers will be turned off by older employees. They believe that customers want young, energetic salespeople, and that their customers will shop elsewhere if they have to deal with an older adult. This thinking comes from the notion that older adults are slower and unable to provide the same level of service as younger workers, that they are not as intellectually adept and not able to provide information as readily, and that they will alienate customers by being unskilled in interpersonal relationships.

Reality: Unretirees Are Often Sought After by Customers Because of Their Attention to Service

In a 1985 study by Yankelovich, Skelly and White of human resource managers, older workers were viewed as possessing experience, skill, and knowledge by 72 percent of the respondents. Morris Massey, in his book *The People Puzzle: Understanding Yourself and Others* (Reston Publishing), reports that older adults generally value tact and diplomacy, while younger workers value candor and honesty.

Older workers are beginning to establish a reputation as providers of stellar customer service and courtesy. Many service industries have begun to seek out older adults because of their consistent provision of excellence in service to the customer.

Fred Marcus, recruitment coordinator for Home Depot, an Atlanta-based chain of home-improvement centers, has found that Home Depot customers "prefer in many instances" to do business with its older employees.[3]

Strategies for Keeping Your Job

- Because of today's emphasis on total quality management (TQM) and excellence in service, be sure to follow your employer's lead on dealing with the customer.
- Be attentive to your customers and ensure that their needs are being met.
- Provide your employers with ideas and suggestions for more effectively meeting customers' needs.

Strategies for Finding a Job

- Stress your background in dealing with customers and with difficult people.
- Provide examples of how you have successfully dealt with difficult people in challenging situations.
- Discuss your values of tact, diplomacy, and courtesy, and demonstrate these qualities during the interview process.

Myth 15: Unretirees Lack Experience

Some employers feel that older adults who do not have a job and who are still in the job market have few marketable skills and little relevant experience. They believe that these job seekers may have lost their job for a reason, or that they lack the necessary qualifications for today's jobs.

Reality: Unretirees Have More Life Experience Than Their Younger Counterparts

Since experience is one of the best teachers, older job seekers are often those with a bounty of experience, judgment, and wisdom. We love the quote from Grace Williams, who said, "We all learn from experience. A man never wakes his second baby just to see it smile." And so it is with older adults, who possess a treasure trove of experience to bring to the workplace.

In today's economy, those older adults in search of a job are often those who opted for an early-out program, who got caught in a rightsizing restructuring, or who were not well suited for their last job. In some cases, older job seekers are merely looking for a way to better their career. In any event, there are a host of individuals with outstanding qualifications that would offer many employers a valuable solution to their staffing dilemmas.

Strategies for Keeping Your Job

- Offer examples of the way your wealth of life experience can benefit your employer on the job.

Strategies for Finding a Job

- Discuss with prospective employers the reasons for your job hunt. Describe the circumstances of your searching for a job.
- Highlight your strengths, both on the résumé and in the interview. Talk about your achievements and about how your life experiences can benefit the employer.

———

You may face many obstacles in your search for unretirement options. Some of the greatest are the misconceptions in the minds of supervisors, hiring managers, human resources professionals, and all those who hold the key to the employment door.

When you want to keep your job or find a new one, be prepared for the stereotypical thinking that still exists in the workplace, understand the truth about your employability, and develop strategies to combat negative thinking on the part of prospective and current employers.

Notes

1. Catherine D. Fyock, *America's Work Force Is Coming of Age: What Every Business Needs to Know to Recruit, Train, Manage, and Retain an Aging Work Force* (Lexington, Mass.: Lexington/Macmillan, 1990), pp. 31–41.
2. David Nye, *Alternative Staffing Strategies* (Washington, D.C.: Bureau of National Affairs, 1988), p. 120.
3. Mary Beth Marklein, "Against the Grain," *AARP Bulletin*, September 1990, pp. 1–5.

Chapter 3

Exploring Your Unretirement Options

Nothing great was ever achieved without enthusiasm.

—Ralph Waldo Emerson

If you're near so-called retirement age, but young and healthy enough not to want to settle for idleness, then this is the time for you to explore new ways to live, earn, and work in your unretirement years.

What are your options for living life fully in your unretirement? Some of these options include the following:

- Keeping your job
- Changing careers
- Arranging one of the new scheduling alternatives
- Taking a sabbatical
- Becoming an entrepreneur
- Volunteering
- Training and retraining

This chapter provides an overview of unretirement options and discusses the pros and cons of each. (The option of keeping your job, changing careers, and training or retraining will also be covered in subsequent chapters.)

"Retirement age" can mean different things to different people. Some people automatically think of age sixty-five when retirement is mentioned. Others think of age sixty-two. Sometimes retirement age is industry-specific. For example, our friend Rick will retire—with full benefits—this year from the police force at age forty. Rick is now considering what his second career will be. Whatever your age, you may have considered retirement and decided, like Rick, that you are not ready to stop working. You have considered and rejected the notion of retirement, and so have made a decision in favor of unretirement. Now let's examine some of those unretirement options.

Keeping Your Job

You may have decided that staying at your present job is the most desirable unretirement option. Doing so gives you the ability to continue on in a field and occupation that is second nature to you, in an industry in which you may have high credibility and a well-established reputation.

If you love your work, find rewards in your career, and can't imagine doing anything else, job retention is the most obvious and logical unretirement alternative. (More information on staying active in your field is given in Chapter 4.)

Pros

- You can capitalize on the career, the company, and the industry that you know and love by continuing your work.
- The possibilities for better salary and benefits are greater if you remain with an employer and don't start over in a new career at the bottom of the ladder.
- You may be able to choose a flexible scheduling option while continuing to work for one employer. Often those who are currently employed stand the greatest chance of negotiating flexible schedules, job sharing, telecommuting, and other alternative work patterns.
- You remain with the work that you know instead of taking a chance on some other career you're not familiar with.

Cons

+ This unretirement alternative doesn't offer you a change, if that is what appeals to you right now.
+ If you are being taken for granted by your current employer, this is not a good option.
+ If you have become stale in your present position, this alternative won't improve the situation.
+ An offer of early retirement from this organization may be too good to pass up, especially if you want to consider other options.

Changing Careers

Are you burned out in your current career but not ready for retirement? Have you always wanted to do something else, but felt that you couldn't explore that path until you received a pension or other income to finance your new beginning? An unexpected early retirement may encourage you to explore another career path that could provide better security or more job satisfaction. Unretirees are finding that second, third, or even fourth careers often meet their needs.

New organizations, such as New York–based Interim Management Corp., are helping unretirees explore career options through a new service they call Executive Tryouts. Try-before-you-buy temporary assignments for executives permit older managers and employers to see if the new assignment is a good one. (Additional information on re-careering is provided in Chapter 5. Chapters 6 and 7 offer information on the job-search process.)

Pros

+ Second careers may provide you with the career you've always dreamed of.
+ A different career path may offer increased job satisfaction, security, or other benefits.

Cons

* A new career direction sometimes means starting at the bottom rung of the ladder in a new field, which usually translates to lower salary, less prestige, and other offsetting consequences.
* Finding a job in a new field can be time-consuming and frustrating. Employers may be reluctant to hire you if you lack experience in the field.

Taking Advantage of the New Scheduling Options

The nine-to-five grind is now being replaced by other options for employees who need flexibility in their schedules. New parents, students, and others trying to balance home and work responsibilities are finding that many organizations now offer varied employment patterns. You too may want to consider these scheduling alternatives. They can offer you more leisure, an opportunity to balance home and work, a chance to work at your own pace, and other benefits. Some of the new scheduling options include:

* *Flexible scheduling* requires that all employees work a core time period. It lets them choose whether to begin work earlier, work later, or follow a traditional nine-to-five schedule—whatever suits them best, as long as they work a regular eight-hour day.
* *Flex-week, flex-month, and flex-year* let employees elect to work a certain number of hours within the week, the month, or the year according to certain guidelines.
* *Job sharing* allows two part-time workers to split a job, acting as a team to complete the requirements of the job.
* *Part-time employment* allows employees to work fewer than eight hours a day, or fewer than forty hours a week.
* *Temporary work* offers the option of working specific assignments, usually to fill in during vacation periods, illness, and for special assignments.
* *Telecommuting* permits employees to work at home, using the telephone, computer, or fax machine.

- *Job shops* are temporary employment agencies for professional and technical occupations.
- *Employee leasing* permits a company to have its employees rehired by an employee leasing company, which then leases the employees back to the original employer for a service fee.

Pros

- Flexible options permit you to balance home and work responsibilities in a creative manner, giving you the freedom to travel, spend time with grandchildren, return to school, or just have time to relax.
- You may be able to negotiate flexible staffing options with your current employer, permitting the company to go on benefiting from your experience and know-how, while enabling you to go on earning a salary and benefits.
- A reduced work schedule may permit you to work in a way that matches your stamina level.

Cons

- Your employer may not offer flexible options. Some employers may be hesitant to begin a new staffing program and may not be able to justify the benefits in view of the costs.
- In part-time, job-sharing, and temporary work options, you may not receive benefits at the same rate as is the case for full-time and standard work patterns. Some organizations, however, are beginning to prorate benefits and offer more competitive benefit packages to employees working less than full-time.

Taking a Sabbatical

Sabbaticals, though still a rarity among U.S. corporations, are being offered by some organizations that want to provide a means for their employees to escape stress and burnout, to take advantage of educational and travel opportunities, to rehearse for retirement, or to just have a change of pace. Sabbaticals offer valuable time off, during which employees can get away from the job and recharge their batteries. Sabbaticals are typically for a six- to twelve-week period, and are offered as frequently as once every four years and as rarely as once during the course of a career.

While sabbaticals are generally offered to tenured college professors, they are only used by about 2.3 percent of companies, reported a 1988 survey by the Conference Board.[1] However, with the graying of America, a few businesses are adding this to their benefit packages. Companies that do provide sabbaticals—among them, Apple Computer, IBM Corporation, Intel Corp., McDonald's Corp., Tandem Computers, Inc., Time Warner, Inc., Wells Fargo & Co., and Xerox Corporation—praise their benefits to both employees and the organization. If a sabbatical appeals to you, why not discuss this with your employer and see what you can negotiate? If you are lucky enough to work for an organization that provides sabbaticals, you will find that they have many benefits.

Pros

* Sabbaticals provide an opportunity to rehearse or try out retirement.
* A sabbatical can give you a chance to return to school to update skills and knowledge or learn a new trade.
* Sabbaticals provide an escape from the stress of working, during which you can recharge your batteries and prepare for returning to the workplace raring to go.
* You can have enough time to travel or explore other interests and hobbies.

Cons

* It is conceivable that an employer might not miss you while you're on sabbatical, thus putting your job in jeopardy. However, it is unlikely that employers offering sabbaticals would have employees taking advantage of this benefit if they jeopardized those who did.

* If you love your job and don't want to be away, this option is not for you!

Becoming an Entrepreneur

Perhaps your lifelong dream has been to begin a business of your own. Whether your dream is to start a small retail establishment, a restaurant, a consulting practice, or a manufacturing venture, your unretirement years may be just the time to explore it. In fact, you may want to consider the concept of looking for customers instead of a new job.

For example, Bob Holmes, who has always loved to cook, found that his job as school superintendent didn't always permit him the time to pursue his love. So when he retired, he decided to make his avocation his new vocation.

He began by studying two hours every day on the subjects of using and raising herbs and flowers. Next, he made numerous calls to research the subject. Today, he sells edible flowers and herbs to restaurants, especially those that feature spa cuisine and the unusual plants that have become his specialty.[2]

There's lots of help available for unretirees wanting to explore the opportunities of self-employment. Two excellent books on the subject, for instance, are: *Blueprint for Success: The Complete Guide to Starting a Business After 50* by Albert Myers (Newcastle Publishing, 1991) and *Start Your Own Business After 50—60—or 70!* by Lauraine Snelling (Bristol Publishing, 1991).

While many individuals have succeeded in building businesses in their unretirement years, others have discovered that the entrepreneurial path is not right for them. And since more businesses fail than succeed, you should carefully explore this option before diving in.

Refer to the list of questions starting on page 53 before setting off on the entrepreneurial path.

Pros

* Fulfilling a lifelong dream can be one of the greatest rewards of pursuing an entrepreneurial venture. Nothing is quite as rewarding as realizing your dream.

- ◆ Entrepreneurship can be financially rewarding—some-times in a big way.
- ◆ You may enjoy the flexibility of being your own boss and running the show your way.

Cons

- ◆ You will need an abundance of time, energy, and enthu-siasm before you can become a successful entrepreneur.
- ◆ Consider the capital necessary to make your dream come true. Are you prepared to bet your finances on your dream?
- ◆ Not everyone is cut out to be an entrepreneur. Be sure to ask yourself the questions starting on page 53 for more information on this unretirement option.

Volunteering

Many of America's communities could not function without the support of their volunteers. And it's not surprising that those who volunteer the most hours per week are older adults sixty-five to seventy-four years of age, offering an average of six hours per week to agencies and organizations that need their services.

Organizations as varied as the American Red Cross, the March of Dimes, and the Salvation Army rely on volunteers to work in clerical, secretarial, professional, and technical-support roles.

The Service Corps of Retired Executives (SCORE) depends on retired and active business people to offer their time to counsel budding entrepreneurs of all ages. Organizations like Pro-Power in Louisville, Kentucky, match professional, execu-tive, and management unretirees interested in volunteering with not-for-profit organizations that need their support. Pro-Power volunteers donate their consulting services to agencies on a part-time basis.

Pros

* If you are interested in a career change, volunteering offers the opportunity to learn more about a chosen field before entering in a paid-work capacity. Along the way, you may receive exposure to excellent training and educational opportunities.
* Volunteering frequently opens doors for unretirees who have found it difficult to find work elsewhere. Volunteer opportunities often become paid-work opportunities once the organization learns it cannot do without your services.
* Volunteering is a way for you to remain active, help others, and act productively.
* Volunteering often permits you more flexibility to take time off for travel, hobbies, and other interests.
* As a volunteer, you are usually much appreciated by the organizations that need you.

Cons

* The most obvious negative is that volunteer work is nonpaid work, at least in terms of cold hard cash. Other important monetary benefits, like insurance, are also not usually offered.
* Just as with other forms of unretirement, not every volunteer position will be right for you, since each position requires a unique set of skills, abilities, and knowledge.

Training and Retraining

Unretirement can provide you with the opportunity to return to the classroom to sharpen old skills and learn new ones. Increasingly, there are special services being offered to arm you with the knowledge you need to survive in an information society.

Many college campuses provide special tuition-free programs for senior citizens. Computer clubs specifically designed for older adults, like the Silver Fox Computer Club in Louisville, Kentucky, are also being offered nationally. SeniorNet, a nonprofit organization based in San Francisco, California, offers a two-month, hands-on training course and a quarterly newsletter for older adults.[3] (An in-depth look at training and development opportunities is provided in Chapter 9.)

Pros

* Training permits you to brush up on rusty and outdated skills so that you'll be better prepared for the workplace.
* Retraining builds self-confidence, especially if you've been out of the job market for a period of time.
* Training may ultimately assist you in earning top dollar upon reentry into the workforce or in receiving that promotion you've been working toward.

Cons

* Time out for training can mean that you are not only not getting paid for work, but may actually need to lay out funds to pay for your instruction.
* Training or retraining activities do not guarantee you a job in today's job market.

Determining What's Best for You

How can you decide which unretirement option or combination of options is right for you? Use the following evaluative questions, exercises, and action strategies to help you choose your best alternatives.

Questions to Ask Yourself

For each of the unretirement options outlined, we've provided some questions to answer before you go further.

General Questions

- Where would I most like to live?
- In what occupation would I most like to work?
- In what kind of work environment would I most like to be?
- What work hours/work schedule would I most like to have?
- What kind of people would I like to have as co-workers? Customers?
- Would I like to travel in my job?
- What gives me greatest satisfaction?

Keeping Your Job

- Do I like or love my job?
- Does this job provide me with the flexibility in scheduling that I need and want? If it doesn't now, would my employer be willing to work with me to provide a flexible scheduling option?
- Do I need the salary and benefits I currently have? Could I earn the same amount in some other field or area?
- What are the pros of this particular job? What are the cons?
- Do I have opportunities to get a promotion or otherwise advance in this job?

Changing Careers

- What occupation or field would I be most interested in?
- Would I be willing to invest my time and money in the necessary training or retraining to make the change?
- How happy am I with my employment situation today? Why would I want a change?
- What are the major reasons I am seeking a change?

Taking Advantage of the New Scheduling Options

- Is my current employer willing to work with me to provide scheduling options? Is there another employer who would provide these options?

- What kind of work schedule am I most interested in having? What needs am I looking to meet in a revised schedule?
- What am I willing to trade in exchange for a more flexible schedule: Salary? Benefits? Status?

Taking a Sabbatical

- Does my employer offer this benefit?
- What would I want to do if I took a sabbatical?
- Would my employer miss my presence? Why or why not?

Becoming an Entrepreneur

- Do I have a unique and marketable product or service?
- Do I have the experience to open a business? What expertise would I need to obtain?
- Am I willing to accept responsibility for my business?
- What kind of time am I realistically willing to put into starting up the business? Running the business?
- Whom can I count on to support me?
- Do I have the financial support necessary?

Volunteering

- What do I like to do?
- Am I willing to work without pay?
- Do I believe in the cause I am supporting?
- Do I like the tasks I will be doing on the job?
- What is my ultimate goal for unretirement? Paid work? Full-time or part-time employment? Employment with the organization with which I am volunteering?

Training and Retraining

- Are my skills, abilities, and knowledge current, given the demands of the workplace today?
- What are the costs of additional training and retraining?

- ◆ Do the benefits of additional training outweigh the costs?
- ◆ What special programs and services are offered in my community?

Exercises for Evaluation

In this section we've provided you with exercises that will assist you in further evaluating the variety of unretirement options available to you.

"Eulogy" Exercise

Imagine that you are attending your own memorial service or funeral and your eulogy is being read. What would be said about you if you were to die today, especially with regard to work/leisure? Next, imagine what you would *like* to hear, and consider the discrepancies between the two.

Career Lifeline Exercise

Take a long piece of paper (you might use a roll of computer paper, or simply tape together several pieces of notebook paper). Then draw a long line horizontally; this represents your life. Mark the line in ten-year increments. Next, consider major life events that occurred during each ten-year segment, and note those on the line. Add your work history (both paid and unpaid). You may also want to note important career decisions and events, risks and obstacles, and future career plans.

If you like, you can post the chart and review it, adding thoughts and ideas. This will give you an overview of your career from which you'll be able to identify interests, trends, and patterns in your life. Use the chart to provide insights about your past as well as your future direction. Ask yourself these questions:

- ◆ What have been my main interests over the years?
- ◆ What skills have I used?
- ◆ Which jobs have I enjoyed the most?

- Where did I feel that my abilities were best used?
- What work patterns are obvious?

(This exercise is adapted from *Counseling Midlife Career Changers* by Loretta J. Bradley.)[4]

Career Fantasy Exercise

Describe a career change you would like to make. Think of something that is within your control but that, for whatever reason, you are afraid to undertake. After identifying the change, answer the following questions. Take out a piece of paper and write down your answers, or discuss them with a friend and brainstorm possibilities. If you have a journal or notebook for charting your unretirement options, you may want to record your ideas and refer to them as you continue your search.

- What is my career fantasy?
- Why does the change appeal to me?
- What would I gain from the change?
- What is frightening about the change?
- What are the obstacles to making this change?
- What is the worst thing that could happen if I make this change?
- What would I do if the worst thing happened?
- What is the best thing that could happen if I make this change?
- What would I do if the best thing happened?
- What would my first step be in pursuing this career fantasy?
- What would my second step be in pursuing this career fantasy?
- What would my third step be in pursuing this career fantasy?

(This exercise is also adapted from *Counseling Midlife Career Changers* by Loretta J. Bradley.)[5]

Action Strategies

For each possible unretirement option, we've outlined action strategies you might wish to explore as you evaluate your unretirement opportunities:

Keeping Your Job

_____ Make sure you understand the performance requirements for your job. Ask for regular performance evaluations to ensure that your work is up to par.

_____ Determine whether your interest is in getting a promotion, staying on in your current job, or working toward a grand achievement. Develop your action strategy for helping you achieve each goal.

Taking a Sabbatical

_____ Find out whether your employer offers sabbaticals. Investigate how the benefit works and what you will need to do to qualify.

_____ Explore the goals you have for a sabbatical. Do you want to study, travel, try out retirement, or just relax?

Changing Careers

_____ Do your homework. Research everything you can about your new career. Find out about the skills, abilities, and experience necessary in the new role. Seek out information interviews with those in the new field to determine compatibility with your background and interests.

_____ Prepare yourself by undertaking any training necessary to update your skills and gain the appropriate knowledge for your new career.

Develop realistic expectations. You cannot expect

to earn at the same level as in your old position unless you have equivalent years of experience, knowledge, training, and ability in the new field.

_____ Make the necessary sacrifices. If this new career path is something you've always wanted to do, why wait any longer, even if it does mean a temporary setback in income, status, or prestige? What is the price of doing what you really love?

_____ Use the smart job-search techniques provided in Chapters 6 and 7 to land the job you want. Network with others to find out about the opportunities in the new arena.

Taking Advantage of the New Scheduling Options

_____ Ask your employer if the company offers flextime, job sharing, telecommuting, or other flexible scheduling options.

_____ Look for a new job that provides you with the flexibility you want.

_____ Talk with those in your network who might have experience with working one or more flexible schedules. Ask them to share their experiences as well as the positives and the negatives of these work options.

Becoming an Entrepreneur

_____ Contact the Service Corps of Retired Executives (SCORE) at 409 Third Street, S.W., Suite 5900, Washington, DC 20024.

_____ Call the Small Business Administration: 202-205-7701.

Volunteering

_____ Make a list of the things you're interested in: the arts, the environment, children, the physically

challenged, the elderly, literacy—whatever in-
spires your concern.

_____ Make a list of the experience, skills, abilities and
talents you possess. Don't forget to include unpaid
work experience and other volunteer activities.

_____ Look in the phone book for organizations that
support your interests. Call directly and let them
know of your interest.

_____ Investigate local volunteer referral centers in your
area by looking in your phone book's white pages
under "volunteer center," "voluntary action center," or "volunteer bureau." For specific groups
that might need help, look in the yellow pages
under "social service organizations." Or write
VOLUNTEER National Center, 111 North 19th
Street, Suite 500, Arlington, VA 22209.

_____ Contact the American Association of Retired Persons' Talent Bank, available to members and non-
members over the age of fifty. To enroll, address a
postcard request to VTB Registration Packet
(D910), AARP Fulfillment (EE104), 1909 K Street
N.W., Washington, DC 20049.

Training and Retraining

_____ Find out what training is available to you in your
community. Contact your local college, university,
vocational institution, or other educational institution to discover what adult education programs are
available and at what cost.

_____ If you need to update your computer skills, visit
your local computer store and inquire about special courses that might be available in the community. Or check out the book *Computers for Kids
Over Sixty* by Greg Kearsley and Mary Furlong.[6]

_____ Contact your local Private Industry Council to determine if you qualify for special training and re-

training programs offered to individuals over age
fifty.

There are a host of unretirement options to choose among—
from keeping your job to changing career directions or working
new schedules; from taking time for a sabbatical to retooling
through an education program; from volunteering with a not-
for-profit organization to becoming your own boss. The decision about how you wish to unretire is up to you and depends
on *your* motivations, *your* interests, and *your* lifestyle. By answering the questions provided in this chapter, following the
exercises, and developing your own action strategy, you can
find your own brand of happiness along the unretirement trail.

Notes

1. Robert Lewis, "Recharging Batteries," *AARP Bulletin*, September
   1991, p. 2.
2. Sarah Fritschner, "A Man Ahead of His Thyme," Louisville *Courier-Journal*, June 13, 1990.
3. Phil Elmer-DeWitt, "Whiz Kids With White Hair," *Time*, February
   12, 1990.
4. Loretta J. Bradley, *Counseling Midlife Career Changers* (Garrett Park,
   Md.: Garrett Park Press, 1990).
5. Ibid.
6. Greg Kearsley and Mary Furlong, *Computers for Kids Over Sixty*
   (Redwood City, Calif.: Addison-Wesley, 1984).

Chapter 4

Staying Active in Your Field

I caught on to the finance stuff really fast. There are things that you like to do, and then there are things that you are very good at. I would love to be a Broadway star, but I am not Bernadette Peters. I *am* very good at finance.

—Deborah A. Coleman, Vice President and CFO, Apple Computer

There is a widespread expectation in the United States of retirement at the age of sixty-five. But you may opt to remain active in your field instead of taking full-time retirement. This is becoming an increasingly popular unretirement option. If you love your career and couldn't imagine life without working in your chosen field, you need to explore ways in which you can work where your passion is.

Ed worked for his high-tech company until he was offered a lucrative early retirement package. His organization was frustrated when they could not replace his skills with new workforce entrants, and returned to Ed to ask him to provide consulting services to the organization. Ed now works part-time as a consultant, making more money than when he worked for the organization as an employee.

Bob worked for over twenty-five years in rotogravure in an occupation that the advent of new technology has now made obsolete. After being encouraged to take a generous early retirement package, he looked for something to keep him active. He tried various jobs but was never quite satisfied with work outside of the printing field. He "missed the smell of the ink" and found happiness when he finally returned to his printing niche in a part-time job with a quick-print shop.

Sue loved her work in the bank as a vice president, but wanted less demanding work as well as more flexible hours that would give her time to spend with her grandchildren, to travel, and to pursue her hobbies. She approached her bank with the idea of working part-time in a service role, and finds that she enjoys still using her banking knowledge while also having the time she needs to pursue other interests.

All these individuals are working within their chosen field, but in a way that satisfies their needs, their motivations, and their interests. Unretirement in the same or a modified position may offer you, too, the kind of experience you want.

Exploring the Options

If you have decided that in spite of expecting to retire at, say, sixty-five, you want something more for your life, there are a number of alternatives open to you. Richard Bolles, the author of *What Color Is Your Parachute?*, offers several options for those individuals whose unretirement decision is to keep their current job. One is to go for that final promotion—to get the recognition that has been earned over time within the organization. A second strategy is to try for a great achievement and outdo a past record. A third option is to survive a difficult period and just hang on to that job during changing and often difficult economic times.[1] (We'll discuss all these alternatives in more detail later in this chapter.)

You may also want to consider unretirement options that permit you to remain within your field, but with another employer. (See Chapters 6 and 7 for job-search strategy information.)

You may define the perfect unretirement as working in your current job with your current employer, only with a modified work schedule. Part-time, temporary, job-sharing, and other flexible options may offer an alternative somewhere between full-time work and full retirement.

Strategies for Staying in Your Current Job or Field

Outlined in this chapter are many of the various unretirement options for remaining in your field, along with considerations for the options and a review of the action strategies to take once you decide upon the right path for you. The information and examples given in this chapter will not only inform you of the many different employment strategies for staying active in your field, but will also give you concrete examples and success stories to use as ammunition in discussions with your employer concerning your work options.

Coasting

Maybe you like your job, or you like your employer, and you just want to continue doing what you've been doing. If you've worked hard and established a stellar reputation, you may well be able to coast along in your job until retirement.

Or perhaps you want to remain with the organization, but in a slightly less demanding role. Xerox, in Rochester, New York, offers unretirees with fifteen years' seniority the opportunity to move to jobs that don't require rotating shifts. They are paid a salary somewhere between their old rate and the rate paid for the less demanding job.[2]

Getting Promoted

Perhaps, having worked hard, you now want the recognition for the outstanding work you've accomplished. Going for that last great promotion opportunity may be the right unretirement strategy for you.

Achieving

Richard Bolles suggests that you have another option—to go for an impressive achievement. The timing may be excellent.

since you can capitalize on your years of experience, your credibility in the field, and your ability to access the right channels and resources. Begin your planning to go for the gold!

Surviving

Perhaps your organization is going through difficult economic times, is restructuring, or is reexamining its operations. Your best strategy in these situations, if you aren't yet ready for retirement, is to simply survive. In these instances, evaluate the organization, be willing to be flexible, and have Plan B available just in case.

Getting on the Grandpa/Grandma Track

In an editorial in *Human Resource Executive*, Allan D. R. Stern and David W. Morris discuss the need for an alternate track for the once-fast-trackers of Wall Street. They cite examples of older executives who are tired of the rat race of up at 5 A.M., off to the exercise club and a power breakfast, then on to the office by 8, work through lunch, and home at 10 P.M. following an after-hours meeting. These executives, they suggest, while not interested in retirement, are now less committed to and motivated by the fast track.

Stern and Morris recommend that, just as corporate America has developed a *mommy track* for those women who want off the fast track for a time while balancing the needs of work and family, there needs to be a *grandpa/grandma track* for executives who aren't yet ready for retirement, but *are* ready to slow down their work pace. Such a track would enable them to use alternative work arrangements to slow down while still remaining strong, contributing members of their organizations.

Corning is one corporation dedicated to offering these options as a means of retaining key managers. The offer of three weeks of unpaid leave with full benefits and job guarantees is one of the ways in which another Fortune 500 company entices its executives to remain with the organization. It also offers home-based work options.[3]

Trying Out Retirement

Perhaps you think you *might* like retirement, but aren't sure if it's the right choice for you today. Increasingly, corporations are offering older adults the opportunity to try out retirement through a phased retirement option.

Kollmorgen Corporation's Electro-Optical Division, in Northampton, Massachusetts, offers its unretirees the opportunity to rehearse retirement by permitting them to work three days for the company, then volunteer with a nonprofit agency for two days. After eight months the employees work two days with Kollmorgen and three days with the agency. By trying this option over a one-year period, older adults can see how they like a reduced-pay work schedule while the company begins to train a replacement. The organization also benefits because its program has won it recognition as a good corporate citizen within the community.[4]

Poloroid Corporation, based in Cambridge, Massachusetts, offers its older workers a chance to rehearse retirement by way of a three-month unpaid leave. The company also lets its unretirees gradually reduce their work hours.[5] Corning, based in Corning, New York, also helps managers and professional employees phase in their retirement over a one- to three-year period by working 40 percent of the time.

Arranging a Flexible Schedule

Flex-week, flex-month, and even flex-year options are being offered by employers across the land. In a study conducted by Towers Perrin, it was found that 50 percent of the companies contacted used some sort of flexible scheduling options.[6]

With flex-scheduling, you can opt to work a certain set of hours or days within the week, month, or year. Companies that allow their employees to set their own schedules have found that their workers are more productive because they have enough time to handle personal business in an appropriate manner.

Companies like Control Data Corporation (CDC) offer all employees the opportunity to work flextime, with a core work period from 10:00 A.M. to 2:00 P.M. each day. Other organizations—such as banks with processing departments for monthly billings—offer unretirees the chance to work part-month or part-year.

Job Sharing

When two employees divide one job between them, job sharing takes place. While job sharing has traditionally occurred in professional and technical businesses, many other industries and occupations are now beginning to offer this option. One study reported that 22 percent of companies are using job sharing for some positions.[7]

If you want to keep working, but on a reduced schedule, you may find that job sharing offers the options you want. Some job-sharing partnerships include an older and a younger employee, with the older job sharer operating in the role of mentor or role model.

Working Part-Time

Employers are now offering less-than-forty-hour schedules for a large number of employee roles, including entry-level as well as professional and managerial positions. A new twist on part-time employment offered by some employers is Voluntary Reduced Work Time, or V-Time. It is being offered by New York State government offices as part of a program to assist employees in working schedules that meet their needs. Another version of V-Time is the Voluntary Reduction in Work Schedule (VRWS) being offered by the New York State Education Department. In this system, employees can work between 70 and 100 percent of their work schedule in 5-percent intervals. If, for example, employees work 80 percent of a full schedule, they receive 80 percent of their salary and retirement benefits, with full health insurance and time-off benefits.[8]

Companies like Aerospace Corp. of southern California, having discovered the advantages of keeping their skilled retirees as part-time workers, have devised a *casual employment* program. Under the program, employees can work up to 1,000 hours each year—about half time—without jeopardizing their pension benefits. About 20 to 30 percent of the Aerospace workers who retire each year return part-time in this program.[9]

Becoming a Temporary Worker

For projects and short-term assignments, employers are turning to temporary employees. While temporary placement agencies are being used to meet many temporary needs, some employers are also exploring the use of contractual workers.

Temporary assignments permit you to try out new employment options, brush up on rusty skills, meet new people, and remain active in your field—all while accepting only those assignments that are of interest to you or that meet your scheduling needs. Many older adults accept assignments when they need some extra cash or funds for a special trip. The ability to accept or reject assignments is appealing to those who need and want time off to pursue other interests.

There are many temporary help agencies actively seeking older adults. A number of agencies, such as Good People in New York City and Retiree Skills, Inc., in Tucson, Arizona, actually specialize in the placement of older adults. Many of the national temporary help agencies are also specifically seeking unretirees to staff temporary assignments. Kelly Services' Encore program and Olsten's Mature Advantage are examples of the special efforts being made to focus on the recruitment of older workers. Temps & Co., a national personnel services corporation, has discovered that unretirees represent the fastest-growing segment of its workforce.[10]

The Travelers Insurance Company's Older Americans Program is one of the best-known part-time employment programs for unretirees. In 1981 it created a job bank for its retirees that acts as an in-house temporary help agency, providing staffing for temporary and part-time assignments within the organization. The program has been so successful that Travelers has expanded the initiative to include any older adult seeking part-time and temporary assignments at its corporate headquarters offices in Connecticut.

Telecommuting

Gaining in popularity are work-at-home arrangements in which the worker does not have to be at the job site the entire work period. Some workers are working one day a week at home; others are working almost entirely out of their homes. With the advent of low-cost office equipment—copiers, fax, computers, modems—telecommuting between employers and employees is becoming more widespread.

Telecommuting can also be an option for older adults who are disabled or who face transportation barriers.

Working for a Job Shop

Job shops are temporary employment agencies for professional and technical occupations. Job shops permit you to put your professional skills and abilities to work without the hassle of independently marketing and bidding each new assignment.

Working for an Employee Leasing Company

Employee leasing companies are becoming popular as companies seek to employ their retirees, but find that pensions are barriers to continued employment. If your previous employer offers a pension benefit that is determined by your earnings over your last work years, then working part-time hours or in a less demanding job at a reduced salary can adversely impact the pension benefits you receive. Working through a leasing company may provide just the answer you need.

These leasing companies hire the employer's workers, and "rent" them to the employer for a fee. Many organizations use leasing companies to rehire retirees or to hire and manage *all* their employees when they don't want the administrative hassles of direct employment.

Leasing companies are most prevalent in California but are catching on across the country. Many temporary help agencies are also acting as leasing companies.

This chapter's opening example was a retiree going back to work for his employer as a consultant and independent contractor—a concept that is gaining in popularity. Employers who find that they cannot readily replace experienced employees are turning to their own retirees for specific services to the organization.

Other retired executives who are interested in unretirement as consultants but who aren't interested in the challenges of establishing an independent business are also seeking the services of organizations such as Interim Management's Executive Tryouts in New York. Operating as an upscale temporary placement agency, this organization permits the individual and the client corporation to work together without the permanent commitment of employment.

Being Rehired

Perhaps you've left the organization for retirement but you've found that you want to return. Or perhaps the organization finds that it cannot do without you. Many retirees are becoming rehirees and returning to their place of employment for full-time, part-time, or other work options.

Questions to Ask Yourself

As an unretiree wishing to remain active within your field, there are a number of factors you will want to consider before choosing the best unretirement options for you.

How Much Time Do You Want to Spend Working?

If you decide to stay active in your field, do you want to work full-time or part-time? On temporary assignments or in a permanent job? Part-year or year-round? Analyze these issues:

- Do I have other priorities in my life that take precedence over work, such as family, travel, hobbies, leisure activities, or volunteer work? What are they? What kind of time will each take? Will it be possible to work and still give the time necessary to these priorities?

- ◆ Do I understand a difference in the benefits, rewards, and challenges of full-time and part-time work in my field? What are the trade-offs? Am I willing to exchange the benefits, rewards, and challenges of full-time employment with those of part-time work?
- ◆ What kind of work schedule will work best? For example, will it be a flex-day, flex-month, or flex-year schedule (assuming that flexible work options are desirable)?
- ◆ Does my current employer offer work-scheduling options? If they haven't in the past, might they be willing to offer such benefits in the future?

What Level of Challenge Are You Seeking in Your Work?

Are you ready to go for a major new challenge, or are you ready to lessen your work responsibilities and relax a bit? Other questions to consider include the following:

- ◆ How hard do you want to work? Need to work? What is the price? What are the benefits? Are the benefits worth the price?
- ◆ How is your health and stamina? Are you physically ready to meet the level of work challenges you seek?
- ◆ Is your current employer able to offer you the level of challenge you seek? Can your goals be realized within your field?

What Level of Risk Are You Willing to Accept?

Each option offers different risk levels. You need to decide what's right for you. Issues to consider include the following:

- ◆ What is the worst thing that could happen? What are the chances it will happen? What will you do if it does happen?
- ◆ What are the benefits for each risk level? Which benefits are most meaningful to you right now? In the near future?

How Much Change Do You Want Right Now?

What are the benefits of each change? Other questions to consider before making a change include the following:

- What will the outcome be if you don't change? What will the outcome be if you do change?
- What resources will you need for the change? What kinds of support?

What Barriers Must You Overcome?

How much do you want the unretirement option? At what price? Here are some other questions to consider:

- Are you facing discrimination or ageism at your current company? How hard must you fight to gain the recognition and rewards you deserve?
- Is your employer already offering flexible schedules? How open is your organization to the kind of alternative schedule you want to work?
- What are the paths being followed by other older adults within your organization and within your industry? Is early retirement the norm? Are there others seeking unretirement options?
- Do you know what you want?

Action Strategies

Outlined here are some ideas for developing your own strategies for staying active in your field as an unretiree.

_____ Decide what you want to do! Review the exercises in Chapter 3 to determine the best option for you right now. Review the questions listed earlier in this chapter to determine the right level of time commitment, change, and risk.

_____ Talk with your employer. What does your company offer currently? What might it be willing to offer? If your current supervisor is a strong ally, discuss your needs and interests with him or her and together decide upon your action strategy.

_____ Outline the barriers that you face. What are they? What resources will you need to overcome these barriers?

_____ Analyze what is happening in your community. Are there other organizations offering unretirement options for their employees? What are the trends? How can you capitalize on these trends?

_____ Explore your network of encouragers and supporters. Who within the organization can assist you? Are there friends in other organizations who might be able to provide support? How can you rally your resources to achieve your goals?

Notes

1. Richard N. Bolles, "The Decade of Decisions," *Modern Maturity*, February–March 1990.
2. Tamar Lewin, "Many Retirees Eagerly Swap Leisure for a Chance to Get Back on the Job," Louisville *Courier-Journal*, April 22, 1990, p. A6.
3. Allan D. R. Stern and David W. Morris, "Executives on the Grandpa Track," *HR Executive*, June 1991, pp. 80–81.
4. Catherine D. Fyock, *America's Work Force Is Coming of Age: What Every Business Needs to Know to Recruit, Train, Manage, and Retain an Aging Work Force* (Lexington, Mass.: Lexington Books/Macmillan, 1990), pp. 193–194.
5. Tamar Lewin, "Many Retirees."
6. *Nation's Business*, November 1990, p. 10.
7. Ibid.
8. Karen Levine, "Flextime—It Works!" *Parents Magazine*, September 1990.
9. Bill Crawford, "Opportunities Knock," *AARP Bulletin*, February 1990, pp. 1, 12.
10. Ibid.

Chapter 5

The Age of Re-Careering: Second Careers, Third Careers, and Beyond

The folly of that impossible precept, "Know thyself"; till it be translated into this partially possible one, "Know what thou canst work at."

—Thomas Carlyle

Re-careering is the new buzzword for work today; some estimates claim we will all have to change our careers up to thirteen times during our lifetimes to keep pace with the changes in technology and industry. And this phenomenon, coupled with the fact that people today are living longer, healthier lives, means that re-careering will probably be a necessary element of unretirement, both today and tomorrow.

Why New Career Directions?

If you have made the decision to choose some form of unretirement over full-time retirement, you should be aware of a number of factors that are creating changes in our perceptions and expectations. Some of these factors are outlined here.

The Changing Nature of Work

It comes as no surprise that high technology has come to dominate industry. Many occupations that were once in great demand are already a thing of the past. But this doesn't mean that you can't find work. (An example of re-careering was seen in Chapter 4, in the example of Bob, who lost his job when the rotogravure process became obsolete, but found work at a quick-print shop.)

Organizational Downsizing

Many businesses are restructuring, or rightsizing, and eliminating outdated or redundant positions in an attempt to stay afloat. Employees of once-stable organizations are finding that they must not only look to new organizations for employment, but also seek new career paths in order to find a position in the corporate world. Employees of General Motors, IBM, and many other large blue-chip companies once believed that they had long-term job security. Thousands of these individuals have been forced to rethink their careers. And, according to a special report in the June-July 1993 *Modern Maturity* magazine, older employees are more often affected by downsizing.

The Desire to Work for Pleasure

Many adults are anxious for retirement because they've been involved in a career they didn't enjoy. After investing years of education and toil in careers that have failed to fully engage their interest and passion, or working for bosses or organizations that have never fully appreciated them, it's not surprising that many Americans actively look forward to retirement.

You may have felt trapped in a career you didn't love, but knew you could not leave because of your years of investment, the high salary you made, the benefits you received, and other variables. However, when retirement arrives, you may realize that you aren't ready to entirely abandon the world of work. You may find that you *are* ready for a job that permits you to love what you are doing.

For some unretirees this means turning an avocation into a vocation; for others it translates into volunteer work; for still others it means opening a business of their own.

The Desire to Do Something Different

Many unretirees discover that it's not so much that they hated their first career, as that they are now ready for something else. Unretirement for you may mean trying your hand at working full-time at a hobby. Or it may offer the opportunity to discover a completely different career path.

The Desire to Move into Paid Work

For those who have spent most of their lives raising children, taking care of the home, or volunteering in charitable organizations, it may be time to get paid for the skills and abilities acquired over a lifetime. Inadequate pension income, high costs of health care, or the desire to finally be recognized as having skills valued in the world of work may be the impetus for seeking a career outside the home.

Re-Careering

Regardless of the reasons, many unretirees are seeking the satisfaction and rewards of a second career, a third career, or beyond. In this chapter we will explore ways to identify skills that can be used in the new career field, resources to help you get there, and action strategies for putting it all together.

If you feel too young for retirement but have taken early retirement, if you've been caught in a rightsizing campaign, or if you're just ready for a change, you may well want to join the ranks of the unretirees who are re-careering.

There are many employers seeking unretirees ready for a re-careering move. One such employer is American Airlines, which is seeking more older flight attendants in an attempt to get a jump on the demographic shift taking place as the baby boomers go gray. American is offering a complete training program, covering safety, security, services, and appearance standards. The travel benefits are especially appealing to many unretirees. (After *Modern Maturity* magazine mentioned the focus of the airline's new recruitment efforts, American received more than 1,000 inquiry letters.)[1]

In an excellent book entitled *The Longevity Factor: The New Reality of Long Careers and How It Can Lead to Richer Lives,* author Lydia Brontë recounts the stories of many people who have successfully re-careered.[2] One of them is David Brown, who is quoted as saying that he became more productive in his seventies than he had ever been before in his life. As Brontë reports, his greatest successes have been achieved in the ten years after age sixty-five. With careers in journalism and publishing behind him, Brown moved his focus to movies and has produced such hit movies as *Jaws, The Sting,* and *A Few Good Men.*[3]

Defining Your Transferable Skills for Re-Careering

How can you determine which re-careering direction is best for you? One way to begin to assess your strengths and abilities is to define your *transferable skills*: the skills you used in one career field that can be applied to another field.

If you were a clerk typist in your first career, you are probably aware that very few offices these days have typewriters. But as you search for a new career, you will realize that your typewriting skills translate into keyboarding skills—skills necessary for many of the high-tech administrative jobs in demand today.

Similarly, if you have nonpaid work experience in organizing charity events or PTA meetings, you may decide that this experience could be helpful in such paid work as planning meetings for associations.

If you were involved in making presentations in your past job, perhaps you could use that experience as a professional speaker or trainer within your chosen field. By understanding what your transferable skills are and how they might be useful to an employer, you'll find that you will be able to sell yourself more effectively in your re-careering search.

Outlined below are five methods for identifying your transferable skills.

Use Action Verbs

Review the list of action verbs listed in Figure 5-1. Read each verb and determine if you have had experience in this area. Be creative and think of examples of both paid and nonpaid work experiences in which you exercised this skill.

On a sheet of paper, write a sentence for each verb, highlighting your accomplishments in this area. Next, think about how you might use this skill in a new field or occupation. Share the list with a friend and brainstorm together.

Once you have created this list, use it again in helping to develop your new résumé, or use the list as a means to prepare for your job interview.

Identify Your Qualities

Your *qualities* are those dimensions of your personality, skills, and experience that are transferable from one career field to another. For example, if you are creative in one career field, you can be creative in another occupation.

Use the listing of qualities in Figure 5-2 to determine where your strengths lie; then think of specific examples in which you used that quality (in either paid or nonpaid work experience). Use the questions after each quality to spur your thinking.

As a next step, use this listing as you did for the action-verb exercise above. Brainstorm ways to use these strengths in other career fields, either independently or with others, and transfer these ideas to your résumé and to discussions on career options with employers.

Create a Functional Résumé

Many unretirees are finding that a functional résumé not only helps them sell their transferable skills in a re-careering move,

(Text continues on page 82)

Figure 5-1. Action verbs.

Mechanical/Outdoor Work

accomplished	diverted	pioneered
approved	eliminated	proposed
assembled	evaluated	rectified
built	fabricated	refined
calculated	fixed	repaired
carried	formulated	reshaped
constructed	handled	resolved
created	identified	restructured
demonstrated	improved	solved
designed	innovated	strengthened
determined	invented	surveyed
developed	investigated	undertook
devised	lifted	
diagnosed	operated	

Scientific/Mathematical Work

accomplished	examined	reshaped
approved	hired	resolved
catalogued	identified	revised
compared	improved	solved
compiled	invented	sorted
computed	investigated	strengthened
conceived	originated	structured
created	pioneered	supervised
demonstrated	presented	surpassed
designed	proposed	undertook
determined	redesigned	
evaluated	refined	

Creative Work/The Arts

accomplished	edited	proposed
arranged	formulated	refined
conceived	identified	reshaped
created	improved	resolved
demonstrated	innovated	solved
designed	invented	structured
developed	originated	undertook
devised	pioneered	wrote

Teaching/Counseling

advised
convinced
counseled
demonstrated
facilitated
fostered
generated
grouped
guided

handled
harmonized
improved
influenced
interviewed
mentored
moderated
monitored
motivated

negotiated
presented
presided
proposed
sponsored
trained
wrote

Managing/Executive Work

accomplished
assured
conducted
controlled
convinced
coordinated
decreased
determined
directed
eliminated
employed
enacted
enlarged
evaluated

examined
exceeded
executed
expanded
generated
hired
identified
improved
increased
influenced
marketed
persuaded
promoted
recruited

rectified
redesigned
represented
retained
revised
scheduled
secured
sold
strengthened
supervised
surpassed
undertook

Accounting/Clerical Work

analyzed
arranged
budgeted
catalogued
compared
compiled
computed
decreased
determined
distributed
employed

enlarged
evaluated
examined
expanded
increased
investigated
maintained
managed
negotiated
organized
planned

produced
proposed
redesigned
reduced
retained
revised
scheduled
supervised
synthesized
systematized
undertook

Figure 5-2. Qualities.

Accountability: Using delegated authority to meet specific responsibilities
Think of a time in which you had to:

- ✦ Take charge of a work group to achieve your goals
- ✦ Organize a group of people to complete a project
- ✦ Manage a large function or event

Assertiveness: Interjecting one's thoughts or actions into a situation
Think of a time in which you had to:

- ✦ Speak up when others were going the wrong way
- ✦ Tell someone that your idea was better
- ✦ Convince a group that they needed to do the job your way

Controlling: Assuring that the plan is followed and the objectives met
Think of a time in which you had to:

- ✦ Orchestrate a complicated plan or project
- ✦ Organize an event or function

Creativity: Developing alternative solutions to problems
Think of a time in which you had to:

- ✦ Come up with a new solution to an old problem
- ✦ Innovate a plan

Decision-Making and Judgment: Selecting the best possible alternative from two or more
Think of a time in which you had to:

- ✦ Make a difficult decision
- ✦ Choose among several action strategies

Delegation: Passing authority to another individual
Think of a time in which you had to:

- ✦ Ask a subordinate to perform a task
- ✦ Follow up with others on their part of an action strategy

Flexibility: Adjusting to changing conditions
Think of a time in which you had to:

- ◆ Change your course of action
- ◆ Make new plans suddenly

Initiative: Taking aggressive and positive action
Think of a time in which you had to:

- ◆ Take control of a situation or people
- ◆ Identify an alternative action stragegy

Leadership: Getting people to work willingly to accomplish an objective
Think of a time in which you had to:

- ◆ Convince others to follow your direction
- ◆ Persuade others to adopt your solution to a problem

Oral Communication: Transferring a thought from one person to another through speech
Think of a time in which you had to:

- ◆ Make a presentation
- ◆ Teach a class
- ◆ Give clear directions so that others could follow

Persuasiveness: Changing another person's view to your own or obtaining a direct commitment from another
Think of a time in which you had to:

- ◆ Convince others that your idea was best
- ◆ Debate your side of the argument
- ◆ Sell others on a new product or service

Planning and Organizing: Outlining a course of action to achieve an objective; structuring and arranging resources to fulfill the plan
Think of a time in which you had to:

- ◆ Create an action strategy for a complex project
- ◆ Plan a multiphase program

Problem Analysis: Identifying the real problem and gathering the necessary information to solve that problem
Think of a time in which you had to:

- ◆ Gather pieces of information in order to make the best decision
- ◆ Sort through a lot of data to determine the relevant information

(continues)

Figure 5-2.   Continued.

Thoroughness: Staying with a task until completion
Think of a time in which you had to:

- Stick with a project when no one else wanted to
- Follow through on a project with many minute details

Written Communication: Transferring a thought from one person to
   another through writing
Think of a time in which you had to:

- Write a clear memo or letter
- Communicate to others through the written word

---

but also helps in the process of determining just what those transferable skills are.

A functional résumé outlines background and experience by functional area instead of according to chronological order. Possible functional headings are offered in Figure 5-3. Review these headings, and outline pertinent experiences, skills, and abilities under each relevant subject. You can use this first as the basis for more in-depth brainstorming about your transferable skills and re-careering options, and then as an aid in developing a functional résumé.

Ask Your Friends

Try this exercise: Go to twenty of your friends, relatives, and business acquaintances. Ask them to provide you with a list of your best skills. Review the list and determine where there are similarities. You may be surprised. One unretiree tried this and found that not one person identified the skills from his first career!

Take a Test

There are a number of test batteries that will identify your personality traits, skills, aptitudes, and career interests. Talk with a career counselor, placement professional, or outplacement counselor about these instruments and decide which will best assist you in determining your re-careering direction. (A listing of assessment instruments is provided in Figure 5-4.)

Resources for Assistance

Schools

If you are a graduate of a vocational school or a university or if you are enrolled in classes at an institution of higher learning, you may have access to excellent vocational counseling services.

Many schools now have on staff an individual who represents the needs of nontraditional students, including older students. These programs often provide testing, guidance, and counseling, and can identify special services for which you may be eligible.

If you are considering enrollment in a school as part of your strategy for re-careering, consult with the professional staff to discover what programs are available to unretirees. Many schools offer free tuition programs, special classes, and other perks for their older students.

Career Counselors

Perhaps you feel lost and don't know where to turn. There are many professionals with education and training in career counseling who can provide assistance. Services can include personality, aptitude, and preference testing, job-search strategy planning, help in creating a dynamite résumé, assistance with interviewing skills, and other services.

There are also counseling services like Second Career, begun by John Bilhartz and offered in conjunction with Virginia Commonwealth University's Center on Aging. Program participants meet in groups for weekly sessions. There is no charge for the program, except a minimal charge for test material. For

(Text continues on page 86)

Figure 5-3.   Functional headings.

Mechanical/Outdoor Work

construction
design
drafting
electronics
engineering
graphic design
inspecting
investigation
layout
management

materials handling
organization
planning
printing
product development
production
programming
scheduling
supervision

Scientific/Mathematical Work

aviation
chemistry
construction
design
electronics
engineering
graphic design
inspecting
instruction
investigation
layout

management
medicine
organization
planning
presentations
program development
public speaking
research
scheduling
supervision

Creative Work/The Arts

advertising
architecture
communications
construction
culinary
design
drafting
editing
instruction
layout
planning

presentations
printing
product development
production
programming
promotion
publicity
retailing
scheduling
supervision
writing

Teaching/Counseling

career development
communication
counseling
employment
instruction
interviewing
management
planning
presentations
program development
programming

public relations
public speaking
research
scheduling
selling
social work
supervision
teaching
testing
training

Managing/Executive Work

administrative
advertising
communications
community affairs
design
employment
finance
fund-raising
instruction
interviewing
investigation
investment
legal

management
market research
organization
planning
presentations
program development
promotion
public speaking
purchasing
real estate
research
selling

Accounting/Clerical Work

accounting
administrative
communication
data processing
drafting
employment
finance
fund-raising
investigation

investment
organization
planning
programming
research
retailing
scheduling
secretarial
supervision

Figure 5-4. Test instruments for determining your re-careering direction.

Vocational Preferences

Holland's Self-Directed Search. This is a test which can be self-administered. It is based on six personality types that are matched with occupational groups, helping people understand the nature of their interests and the occupations in which they might be interested.

The Strong-Campbell Interest Inventory. This is an interest assessment that focuses on likes or dislikes regarding specific occupations. It utilizes Holland's six personality types.

Aptitudes

The General Aptitude Test Battery (GATB). This instrument was originally used by the United States Employment Service for career counseling and placement in state employment offices.

The Armed Services Vocational Aptitude Battery (ASVAB). This test was developed for use in the military services and has become the vocational test most often used today in secondary schools.

Personality

Sixteen Personality Factor Questionnaire (16PF). This is an often used instrument that involves a clinical description of sixteen personality traits.

Myers-Briggs Type Indicator. This personality questionnaire has become the most widely used personality inventory today. Based on Jung's theory of psychological types, it helps people understand themselves and their behaviors.

---

information, contact: Virginia Center on Aging, 1008 East Clay Street, Box 229, MCV Station, Richmond, VA 23298–0001; (804) 786-1525.[4]

Another service offered exclusively to unretirees is the Employment Access for Retirees (EAR), founded by sociologist Arlene Rosenthal in Austin, Texas. The service assists persons over age fifty-five by providing an employer-matching system. The fee for the service is $225 to $350, plus a monthly charge.

In addition, clients are expected to volunteer each week at their office.[5]

You can find career counselors through government-funded employment and training programs at your local state employment office, at vocational schools and universities, through employment agencies, and through outplacement firms. (Use the resource guide in the Appendix to locate services near you.) You may also look in the Yellow Pages under "counseling," "vocational," and "résumé" for professional services in your community.

Outplacement Professionals

Outplacement firms are organizations that provide services to corporations that are laying off employees. The corporation contracts with the outplacement firm to provide counseling services and job-search assistance to key employees, usually at middle-management levels and above, to asist them in their transition back into the workplace.

While these outplacement firms generally provide services only to corporations, some will also offer their services to individuals for a fee. Services can include testing, help with résumé preparation, development of job-search strategies, interviewing skills review, and other related services. Look in your Yellow Pages under "outplacement," or contact your local human resources association or chamber of commerce for additional information.

Strategies for Re-Careering

Retraining

For many re-careering moves it is necessary to obtain training or retraining in the new field. Courses may be offered through government-funded employment and training programs, on-the-job training, volunteering, special classes, or vocational and college programs. (For additional information on training and retraining opportunities, refer to Chapter 9.)

The Job Search

Unless you are volunteering your services to an organization, starting your own business, or retraining and returning to work with your former employer in a new capacity, you'll probably have to return to the job market to search for your new career position. (Refer to Chapters 6 and 7 for information on how to structure your job search, and how to put together the important tools of job search, including the cover letter, the résumé, and the job interview.)

Information Interviewing

The information interview can be an important tool when you are considering re-careering options. (Chapter 6 provides additional information on using the information interview to help begin the search for a new career.)

Networking

One of the most critical components of the job search process is networking, and its importance cannot be overstated. *Networking* is based on the theory that the more people who know about your job search, the better your chances of finding a job. Many—if not most—positions are found through networking. Some experts say that 80 to 90 percent of jobs are filled through the "hidden job market" of unadvertised jobs.

Begin with a running list of names to contact. Start with the obvious: family, friends, neighbors, co-workers, former co-workers, and your holiday card list. Then see how far you can expand this list, using friends of your parents, friends of your siblings, parents of your children's friends, acquaintances, your banker, your accountant, friends of your friends, and so on. Put the list aside for a few hours, and then come back to it and see how many more names you can add. This is your network. These are the people to contact to get the word out about your job search and what sort of job you are looking for. You might want to give each of them one of your unretirement cards (described in the next section).

Helen Axel, an employment analyst at the Conference Board, a New York–based business research group, says that "The best jobs are filled through word of mouth, through networking." She goes on to say that older workers have an advantage here because they have a wider circle of job-related contacts than young people who are just starting a career.[6]

In discovering a new career and landing a job, your success may well depend, not just on whom you know, but on how many people you know. In a recent study conducted by a University of Southern California professor, it was discovered that for job seekers over the age of fifty-five, the greater the number of people known, the more favorable the impact on the job search.[7]

The Unretirement Card

A tool that many job seekers are using is an enlarged business card that can be passed along to friends, associates, and those they meet. This card includes contact information along with a brief synopsis of qualifications and area of interest. The card is a convenient way to pass along information to those who might be able to provide you with the right connection for the next career move. (Refer to Figure 5-5 for an example of how an

Figure 5-5. The unretirement card.

John Smith
Home: (555) 222-3456
Work: (555) 333-4567

Job Objective: Sales Position

Qualifications: More than ten years of retail sales experience. Proven ability to work well with others and supervise and manage the work of employees. Experienced with mainframe and personal computer applications, including Lotus 1-2-3, WordPerfect, and other software.

Excellent interpersonal and written communication skills.

unretiree with a sales background might develop an unretirement card.)

Job Clubs and Success Teams

A powerful tool for unretirees is a job club or success team.
The term *success team* was popularized by the book *Wishcraft* by
authors Barbara Sher and Annie Gottlieb, who encouraged
people to get together to discuss their dreams and support
each other in pursuit of those dreams.[8]

A job club or success team meets regularly (usually at least
once a week) and can be facilitated by a career counselor or
other placement professional. The purpose of a job club is to
give the job seeker information on the labor market, assess
strengths of the individual, jointly develop job-search strategies, and benefit from the shared experiences of job seekers.
Often, graduates of the program—those who have found employment—come back as a resource to provide information or
just encouragement.

While it is impossible to know exactly how many success
teams there are, organizers believe that there are more than
1,000 across the country. There are also many job clubs that
are being organized exclusively for older adults. Find out if a
job club is available in your community by contacting the state
employment office, the state office on aging in your state, a
local program offering employment services for older adults,
or your chamber of commerce. (Consult the resource guide in
the Appendix for contact information.) To find a success team
near you, send a self-addressed, stamped envelope to: Wishcraft and Success Teams, Box 20052, Park West Station, New
York, NY 10025.

Re-careering is not only an appealing unretirement option for
many older adults, but often a necessary one. It can offer you
the opportunity to strike out in a direction that meets your
needs, challenges your mind, and fulfills your desire for work
that is satisfying.

Re-careering options—including volunteering, starting your own business, or finding that second or third career or beyond—offer exciting challenges for unretirees. By identifying the skills that can be used in a new career field, the resources to help you get there, and action strategies for putting them all together, you'll be on the road to fulfilling the *new* American dream.

Notes

1. Evan Ramstad, "American Airlines Recruits Older Flight Attendants," Louisville *Courier-Journal*, August 5, 1991, p. B6.
2. Lydia Brontë, *The Longevity Factor: The New Reality of Long Careers and How It Can Lead to Richer Lives* (New York: HarperCollins, 1993).
3. Ibid.
4. "Helping New Careers Take Shape," *NCOA Networks*, April 13, 1990, vol. 2, no. 2.
5. Ibid.
6. Robert Lewis, "Networking: New Tactics Lift Older Job Seekers," *AARP Bulletin*, February 1993, p. 1.
7. "Social Network Size Matters, Jobs Study Shows," *Modern Maturity*, August–September 1992, p. 8.
8. Barbara Sher, with Annie Gottlieb, *Wishcraft: How to Get What You Really Want* (New York: Ballantine Books, 1979).

Chapter 6

The Job Search: Preparing Your Job-Search Strategy

> Your possibilities are limited only by your imagination and drive. But whatever you choose to do, don't scrap your history; rather, build on your skills, experience, and accomplishments.
>
> —Robbie Miller Kaplan, *The Whole Career Sourcebook*

It's been said that looking for a job is one of the most difficult jobs you'll ever have—and it's true! In working with many older adults who want to enter or re-enter the job market, we often hear about the difficulties jobseekers have in overcoming age bias and sharpening or developing their job-search skills.

For example, you may never have actually searched for a job before. (We have counseled many people who got their first job twenty, thirty or more years ago through someone they knew, and so have never had to go through a formal job-search process.) Or you may never have worked before. Or perhaps you *have* gone through the job-search process sometime in the past, but your job-search skills are now rusty. Or perhaps you feel that it's hopelessly difficult to compete with younger job seekers who have received recent counseling and job-search advice.

There is a set of procedures you can follow to gain access to that all-important job interview. It's like learning the combination to a lock. Once you know the combination and what direction to turn the knob, you can easily open the lock and gain access. In this chapter we'll outline a job-search process that anyone, at any age, can follow. We will also provide tips and techniques that apply specifically to the older job seeker.

Beginning the Job Search: Mapping Out Your Plan

You would never think about going on a trip without first looking at a map to determine where you wanted to go and determining the best way to get there. Yet when people begin the job-search process, they often fail to consider this most important planning part of the process.

Crucial planning elements of the job search include a close examination of the labor market and a decision about where to look for employment as well as an assessment of the talents, skills, and abilities you have to offer an employer.

Where to Look for Employment

Consider for a moment your network—those connections with the people you have worked with, socialized with, gone to church with, and know through the various activities and organizations you are involved in. Your network offers you a wealth of job-search information, information that positions you far better than most young job seekers looking for their first job. Most first-time job seekers have only a small network of friends, acquaintances, and family who can assist them in finding a job. You have an advantage in the job market: the connections you have established through years of working and living.

Who is in your network? Here's a checklist of the types of contacts to review for ideas on identifying your job-search connections.

_____   Previous supervisors

_____   Previous co-workers

_____   Neighbors (past and current)

_____   Family members

_____ Professional acquaintances (vendors, clients, professional colleagues, members of professional/trade associations)

_____ Social acquaintances (club members, fellow hobbyists, friends of friends, friends of family members)

_____ Christmas/holiday/birthday card list

_____ Church acquaintances

What else should you consider in developing your road map of where to look for employment? Identify what companies are looking for employees by reading the newspaper for help-wanted advertisements (though it must be remembered that many jobs are filled without placing an ad) and for articles on business expansions, new product lines, and large contracts. Call your chamber of commerce for information on businesses relocating in your community.

Use your network of contacts to learn more about the labor market climate in your area. Call past co-workers to learn about their new place of employment; contact your old boss to ask about opportunities at his or her organization; attend an association meeting to listen to what's new in your community. In other words, gather as much information as you can about what is happening in the employment arena so that you can appropriately plan your job-search activities.

Another tip for your job search: Look for employers who have made a commitment to hiring unretirees, or who have communicated an interest in hiring older workers. The names of many employers who are anxious to hire mature workers are included in this book. You can also be on the lookout for articles about such employers in your local newspaper or place telephone calls to your local chamber of commerce, senior citizens center, or your state employment office to get the names of employers looking for job candidates with experience.

Some temporary help agencies focus exclusively on placing older adults in temporary jobs. Other national temporary help agencies, such as Kelly Services, have communicated their interest in hiring more unretirees through their Encore initiative. Olsten Temporary Services also recognizes the value of maturity and has a special Mature Advantage program.

A number of organizations have made a commitment to hire older adults. One such organization is McDonald's (remember their commercial featuring the older man on his first day of work?), The Travelers Insurance Co., and Honeywell. Also, businesses with a special interest in older adults may seek unretirees. PNC Bank in Louisville, Kentucky, offers Club 55, a retail marketing program targeted to customers over the age of fifty-five, and is also interested in hiring more older employees to provide services to this increasingly important customer base.

Assessing Your Skills and Abilities

Knowing your skills and abilities and the experience you can bring to the job market is essential. Complete the following personal assessment questionnaire to determine what you have to bring to the employment table.

Personal Assessment Questionnaire

What are my skills? _____

What are my talents? _____

What is my knowledge base? _____

What are my hobbies? _____

What do my friends call on me to do? _____

Where have I had successes in my career in the past? _____

Where have I had failures in my career in the past? _____

What are my strengths? _____

What are my weaknesses? _____

What gives me satisfaction? _____

What frustrates me? _____

What kind of lifestyle do I want? _____

What lifestyle do I have now? _____

What will I need to do to improve my situation? _____

In what situations do I have the most self-confidence? _____

What are my immediate goals? _____

What are my long-term goals? _____

What am I willing to do to achieve my goals? _____

Job-Search Activities

Finding a job is a lot like selling a product. The most successful salespeople are those who get out there and make lots of sales calls. It's a numbers game, with those who make the most sales calls making the most sales. In fact, a friend of ours, Joe Bonura, a sales trainer and professional speaker, has said that the three keys to successful selling are: (1) make calls, (2) make more calls, and (3) make many more calls. The same holds true in looking for a job. The more contacts you make regarding employment, the better the opportunity to get a job.

Inertia can be a powerful force to overcome in the job-search process. You may feel it's difficult to begin the process bcause you fear failure, lack knowledge about the process or the results, or aren't sure what might be the best first step to take. The best thing to do is to *do something!*

Here is a checklist that will assist you in determining which steps to take as you begin your job search.

Job-Search Activity Checklist

_____ Talk with a friend about a job
_____ Talk to a relative about a job
_____ Talk to a connection about a job
_____ Talk to an acquaintance about a job
_____ Follow up on a conversation about a job

_____ Walk in and inquire about a job

_____ Walk in and complete an application

_____ Follow up on an application

_____ Contact a community organization about a job

_____ Contact an agency about a job

_____ Follow up on a contact

_____ Read the newspaper for help-wanted ads

_____ Call on a help-wanted ad

_____ Apply on a help-wanted ad

_____ Look in the Yellow Pages for companies to call upon

_____ Call a company for a job

_____ Go to the library to research companies

_____ Investigate upgrading your education

_____ Apply to a school for education or training

_____ Contact your school placement office about careers

_____ Design a résumé and cover letter

_____ Print your résumés

_____ Mail your résumés

_____ Attend a career fair

_____ Attend an open house

_____ Listen to the radio and television for recruitment messages

_____ Watch billboards for recruitment messages

_____ Watch for point-of-sale recruitment messages

_____ Look on community bulletin boards at the bank, grocery store, laundromat, and church for recruitment messages

_____ Check your community newspapers for recruitment ads

_____ Network with your professional/technical association

_____ Read your trade or technical publications for recruitment advertisements

_____ Look for recruitment messages in general-interest
publications

As you begin the job-search process, it will be helpful if
you keep a notebook or journal to record and track your
activities. Each time you make a call, or follow up on a job
lead, record it in your notebook. This will help you in determining when it is time to make a follow-up call on that résumé,
or check on information your friend was going to give to you.

Also, make a commitment to do *some* job-search activity
each day, and add something in your journal daily. By continuing to generate activity, you can substantially increase your
chances of finding the right job.

The Information Interview

One job-search activity being used extensively is the information interview. An *information interview* is a meeting between a
job seeker and an employer representative in which the job
seeker asks questions about careers within the industry as well
as advice on how to gain access to job openings. The information interview puts the job seeker in the role of the interviewer
asking questions that will help him or her in the job-search
process.

The information interview is *not* a job interview. In fact,
many employers are unwilling to participate in information
interviews because some desperate job seekers have secured
an information interview only to turn the tables during the
process and ask for a job. However, in some instances—when
the *employer* chooses to turn the tables—the information interview can become a real job interview.

The information interview has several advantages:

1. It generates less tension for you, because *you* are the
interviewer.

2. It provides a relaxed forum for gathering information about new career areas.
3. It is a good way of building a network that you can use even after you get your job.
4. It is a good way for you to begin to see that all interviews are a two-way exchange of information.

Here are some guidelines for developing a productive, successful information interview.

1. *Identify the right person for the interview.* Ideally, you should not target the human resources professional for your information interview unless your job search is for a position in the human resources field. Find out, before calling to set up your appointment, who the head of the department is within your area of expertise or interest so that you can direct your inquiry to that individual.

2. *Explain the purpose of your call and let the individual know how much time you are requesting.* Some people aren't familiar with the information interview and may need to know what you are asking for. You can start the conversation saying something like, "I'm beginning my job search in a new career direction, and I'm very interested in working in marketing. I understand that you are [title], and I'd like to meet with you for about twenty minutes to ask you some questions about how you got into the field, how you like your work, and so forth. It would help me a lot in choosing my career path. Would you be available for a twenty-minute meeting sometime this week?" Let your contact know that you plan to take up as little of his or her time as possible and that you will honor your time commitment.

3. *Be prompt or early; if you're not sure on directions, do your homework.* With younger adult job seekers, it is imperative to belabor this point. However, with older adults, employers say that the opposite is usually true, and that the main problem is that older adults often arrive for appointments anywhere from fifteen minutes to an hour early! The target for arriving early should be in the five-to-ten-minute-early window. It is impor-

tant to be prompt and show as much courtesy to the employer as possible, since this is a request for his or her valuable time.

4. *Come prepared with your questions; it's OK to have them neatly written in a notebook or portfolio.* In most of the information interviews where we've been on the other side of the desk, the job seekers have had all their questions prepared in advance so that they haven't wasted one valuable minute. Here are some questions typically asked in the information interview; tailor these to meet your needs:

- How did you get into this field? (Note: This is a great one to get them talking.)
- What is a typical day like for you?
- What do you like best about this job? Least?
- What are the job satisfactions? Dissatisfactions?
- How do individuals typically get into this field? This industry? This company?
- What advice would you give to someone like me in the job-search process?
- What training, education, and experience is important for me to have to move into this career?
- Who else should I talk with in order to gather information that will help me in my job search?
- Who do you know of who is looking for someone like me?

5. *Takes notes.* You'll want to remember specific information. Use a notepad to jot down key information, including contact names, addresses, and telephone numbers.

6. *Dress for the job; look like a pro!* Since many information interviews can become *real* interviews, be prepared and dress as you would for a job interview. Your host may even want to refer you to someone else in the organization after your information interview, so it's best to be prepared! A good rule of thumb is to dress as those do on the job, or at one level above the job. You can get an idea about the kind of attire typical for the organization by observing employees on their lunch hour or as they arrive or leave each day.

7. *Be prepared for a real interview; many times an information interview can become a job interview.* Remember, you yourself should never turn the information interview into a job interview because your host may feel that you weren't totally honest in your request for time together. However, if your *host* chooses to turn the information interview into a job interview, be prepared. (Refer to the section in Chapter 7 on preparing for a job interview.)

8. *Watch your time and honor your commitment.* If you asked for twenty minutes when you scheduled the interview, it's important that you honor your time commitment. One information interviewer used his digital watch to time the twenty minutes allotted, and when the alarm went off he stated that he had asked for twenty minutes, and now that the time was up wanted to honor that request. The host was so impressed that she insisted they spend some additional time talking together. Another information interviewer simply looked at her watch when the time was up, and let the host know that she appreciated and valued the time that had been given her. The host also spent additional time with this courteous individual.

9. *Ask for referrals, both for jobs and for other sources of information.* Since one purpose of the information interview is to gain additional job-search information, it's important to ask questions that will continue to help you in your job search. Ask for the names and numbers of others who might be able to assist you by providing you with further information, or those who have job openings available in your field.

10. *Keep the interview on track, unless, of course, the information interview is becoming a job interview.* Some individuals may get off the track (by talking endlessly about how they got into the business, for instance). However, since you've asked for a certain amount of tme and you want to honor that commitment, it may be necessary to say something like, "This is really interesting, but since we only have twenty minutes together, I'd like to cover this next issue."

11. *When the interview is over, thank your host for his or her time, then follow up with a thank-you note.* We find it amazing to

hear how few people receive thank-you notes from the people they have met with. By sending thank-you notes, you not only say that you appreciate others' help and respect their time, but also that you are a dependable individual who knows how to follow up—all important elements in the reputation you want to develop. Such thank-you notes can be handwritten as long as they are legible, neat, and free of misspelled words.

12. *Follow up any leads or referrals given to you—the sooner the better.* If you've received a lead on a job or on someone with whom you might conduct another information interview, follow it up as soon as possible. A good lead is usually only good for a short period of time, since a good lead is probably one that is known by others. Also, people change jobs, move away, or leave their current employers. Follow up quickly to get the maximum benefit from your new connections.

Backdoor Strategies: Part-Time, Temporary, and Volunteer Work

Many individuals find that job-search activities are a major drain on their energy and on their self-esteem and confidence. For these individuals, getting a job by going in the back way may be the best way to get that foot in the door. Excellent backdoor strategies include part-time work, temporary work, and volunteer assignments.

Some unretirees find that part-time work provides an outlet for creative talents, some additional income, and the opportunity for socialization. However, part-time work may also be the way to make a transition to increased hours or to full-time employment. Accepting part-time employment may provide an opportunity to brush up on rusty skills and abilities, learn new skills, and become proficient enough to secure the desired employment opportunity.

Temporary work assignments may be another way to make the transition to permanent part-time or full-time employment. For example, at Kentucky Fried Chicken, we often brought in temporary employees through a temporary help agency, only to find that we wanted and needed the services of the individual as a regular employee. By getting to know the individual first as a temporary, we could ensure that he or she would meet our performance standards before we offered him or her a full-time job. This is typical of many companies today.

Anne's Story

When I reentered the job market after not working outside of my home for nearly twenty years, my first job was as a secretary with a temporary service. I worked as a temporary for four years and it was a wonderful experience. I sharpened my skills, gained a great deal of much-needed self-confidence and worked when it suited me. For example, I never worked between Thanksgiving and Christmas, but usually would accept an assignment after the holidays were over!

I was offered several permanent jobs while on temporary assignments, and finally accepted a permanent secretarial position, after having worked with the company for six months. This job started me on my career path to my final position with the organization as a trust officer and human resources professional. Speaking from my own personal experience, I highly recommend this route.

Many temporary help agencies across the country offer assistance to retirees. Further, some companies, like The Travelers Insurance Company in Hartford, Connecticut, have created a pool of temporary workers that is composed of retired individuals. These temporary employees work on specific assignments, such as vacation fill-ins, special projects and assignments, and on long-term vacancies due to the illness or disability of staff members.

You may find that volunteering is the perfect outlet for sharpening your skills and getting a foot in the employment door simultaneously. By working in an organization on a voluntary basis you learn the policies, procedures, and players, as well as specific job skills. And, if you do well at your job, the organization may want to hire you on a full-time or part-time basis to keep your expertise. (More information on part-time work, temporary employment, volunteering, and other work options is highlighted in Chapter 4.)

Positioning Yourself for Success

Selling yourself to an employer may be difficult. You may have been taught that it is inappropriate to talk about yourself, or brag about your qualities and attributes. You may also feel that you don't have a lot to offer compared to a younger worker. Or perhaps you are unsure about what you have to offer, or can't see how your abilities might transfer to on-the-job skills.

Whatever your hesitation, get over it! Employers continue to say that one of the most important things they look for in a job applicant is attitude. In fact, most have said that you can teach individuals how to perform specific tasks, but it is impossible to teach anyone how to have the kind of positive outlook that will be an asset to the organization.

So, what can you do to position yourself for success in the job-search process? Here are some guidelines for maintaining a good attitude and making a favorable impression:

1. *If you act like a winner, you'll feel like a winner!* Enter the job-search process believing that you will find the best job for you. Since positive expectations bring positive results, expect the best.

2. *You have something to offer; find out what it is and be prepared to offer it to an employer.* Do your homework and prepare for the job-search process as we've already discussed. Ask yourself the questions in the Personal Assessment Questionnaire earlier in this chapter, and be prepared to discuss your strengths and abilities with an employer.

3. *Show that you have a winning attitude!* As you network with friends, family, and neighbors (and everyone you can

think of), be sure to keep your positive attitude in place. Sometimes this is difficult, but it is always important.

4. *Be ready to talk about your strengths; don't be afraid to sell yourself.* Keep your strengths, abilities, and talents in mind and don't be afraid to talk about them as you network. If you need to first believe this yourself, then by all means work on your beliefs until you can honestly sell yourself to others.

5. *Don't appear desperate for a job.* Although you may feel desperate, desperation is not a good selling tool even with your friends and certainly not with a prospective employer. In fact, many employers avoid people who seem too desperate for a job. The rationale: Desperate job seekers may settle for a job in which they are ultimately dissatisfied, causing lower productivity, morale, and often, turnover. Focus on achieving a good match between your strengths and abilities and those needed on a job.

6. *Dress for success.* Whether you are preparing for an information interview or a job interview, be sure to dress appropriately. This means a neat, clean appearance, with clothing selected that is right for the industry, the company, and the job level.

———

Planning for the job search can be one of the hardest jobs you'll ever have. However, by assessing your network, doing your homework on companies to target, evaluating your strengths and abilities, and mapping out your job-search strategy, you'll fare far better in your competition for the best jobs.

Chapter 7

The Job Search: Cover Letters, Résumés, Applications, and Interviews

If you wish in this world to advance,
Your merits you're bound to enhance;
You must stir it and stump it,
And blow your own trumpet,
Or trust me, you haven't a chance.

—William S. Gilbert, English playwright

Just as a salesperson needs sales literature and marketing materials to sell products, you need the tools of the trade to sell yourself to prospective employers. What are the marketing materials that will help you sell yourself? The cover letter, résumé, and application form are the sales literature that will help move you closer to a job opportunity, and the interview is the sales call that will close the sale.

The Cover Letter

All résumés should be sent with a cover letter to ensure that the résumé is considered for the appropriate position, and to increase its chances of being read. The cover letter also directs the résumé to the individual who is responsible for reviewing résumés and scheduling interviews.

Consider these suggestions for developing a cover letter that will get your résumé noticed:

- Make it simple, brief, and easy to read. Remember that the hiring manager has many résumés to review.
- Cover key points, such as your major accomplishments or ways in which your background meets the requirements for the job—bullets are excellent and make the cover letter easy to read.
- Sell your background, skills, and abilities by translating these facts into features and benefits for the employer to show how your background meets the requirements for the job and how it can benefit the employer.
- Address your cover letter to a specific person, and refer to the specific job that you seek by title.
- Entice the reader to read on—and to call you for the interview.

There are three crucial points to be included in the cover letter. The first point tells the reader what you are applying for and directs the résumé to the appropriate person. The second briefly describes why you should be considered and highlights your background, education, and abilities and skills. The third point tells the reader what action you will take. See the sample letter in Figure 7-1.

The Résumé

The résumé is perhaps your most important sales and marketing tool, as it allows you to organize your work experience in a way that shows off your best attributes. While a résumé alone will usually not get the job for you, it is a tool that helps to get your foot in the employment door by securing a job interview.

Obviously, your name, address, and telephone number need to be prominently displayed on the résumé. With the advent of telephone answering machines and voice mail, job

Figure 7-1. Sample cover letter.

June 12, 1994

123 West Main Street
Louisville, KY 40202

Mr. John Smith, Director
Human Resources Department
General Electric Company
Appliance Park
Louisville, KY 40225

Dear Mr. Smith:

I have read in *Business First* about your expanding Human Resources Department and am interested in the open position of trainer which you advertised in Sunday's *Courier-Journal*.

As you can see from my enclosed résumé, my background involves ten years of progressive experience in Human Resources, with special emphasis in the training function. I believe that my past accomplishments of organizing and developing a successful training department from the ground up could provide a real benefit to your department and your company.

I will call you the first of the week to discuss making an appointment for an interview. I look forward to talking with you then.

Regards,

Mary Jane Johnson

---

seekers can easily receive messages from interested employers. If you don't have an answering machine, then by all means list as a backup the number of some reliable person who can forward messages from interested employers to you.

What comes next in the résumé depends on you and your experience. If you have just completed a degree or have taken some courses in a related field, perhaps that information should be stated first. If, however, you have a very strong background in the field for which you are applying, then that information should come first. Since many employers will not have the time to read every word of your résumé, you should structure it to highlight the most important information first so that it will be read.

Some older adults have asked us whether or not to include dates on their résumé, as dates can be a dead giveaway as to the age of the job seeker. Our response: Include only such information as can be viewed as a positive by employers. If you've worked for one employer for a number of years, it might be best to show the number of years worked for that employer as opposed to the exact dates of employment (although this information will usually be requested on the application form). Remember, too, that hiring managers are looking for ways to screen out résumés, leaving only the best and most highly qualified individuals. Eliminate whatever information might cause your résumé to be weeded out.

In some cases, the inclusion of dates might be a positive. For example, if you've just gone back to school and received a degree, placing those dates on your résumé could be seen as distinctly positive. However, if your education was completed prior to the 1980s, it is best to eliminate that information for purposes of the résumé. Figure 7-2 shows a sample résumé.

Using Your Résumé: The Call-Letter-Call Strategy

Many job seekers have been disappointed after sending out a mass mailing of their résumé to employers. If a company does not have a current employment need, the résumé is often not even considered. Some companies only accept résumés and

Figure 7-2.   Sample résumé.

ANNE M. DORTON
P.O. Box 905
Prospect, Kentucky 40059
(502) 228-3869

EDUCATION

* Master of Education in Counseling, 1989, University of Louisville. Grade point average 4.0.
* Bachelor of Arts in Psychology, 1987, University of Louisville. Graduated with honors.

EXPERIENCE

Human Resources

* Created training study course and testing for support staff
* Interviewed and hired new staff; wrote performance appraisals and determined promotions; took disciplinary action as needed
* Compiled job descriptions and procedures manual and kept all human resources records

Counseling

* Conducted individual and group counseling with unemployed, underemployed, and visually impaired individuals
* Administered work sample tests, interest inventories, 16PF, and ability assessments

Administrative

* Established and maintained all office procedures for new small business
* Directly supervised the work of over thirty administrative support staff
* Exceptional verbal and written skills

WORK HISTORY

Innovative Management Concepts
Vice President

March 1989 – Present

First Kentucky Trust Company
Trust Officer
April 1977 – August 1985

Note from Anne: I received my master's degree in vocational counseling in 1989, and because this is so recent (and shows my ability to learn) I always put it in a conspicuous place on my résumé and include the date. I also add that my grade point average was 4.0.

applications when they have specific openings and discard all unsolicited applications and résumés at other times. A better approach is to follow the *call-letter-call* strategy used by many salespeople. This approach involves calling a company first to determine interest; next, sending a résumé with a cover letter addressed to the appropriate hiring authority; and finally, making a follow-up call to schedule an interview.

The Application Form

The application form is another important element in your job search, and deserves your careful attention.

Most companies ask prospective employees to complete an application form prior to an interview. It is used to check for consistency between it, your résumé, and the interview (dates, titles, responsibilities, reasons for leaving, etc.). This ensures that the job candidate is honestly presenting information. Since it is difficult to remember exact dates, places, and other employment information, you can ensure the accuracy of what you write and say by using a *cheat sheet*—a list of all your employment data—when filling out the application. A cheat sheet will also help speed up the time it takes you to complete the application form. A sample of a cheat sheet is shown in Figure 7-3.

The employer is also looking to see if the application is complete and trying to identify missing information. For example, if dates are missing, the employer may attempt to discover if there is a gap in employment, or if you are trying to hide a negative aspect of your employment history. You can

Figure 7-3.   Cheat sheet.

General

Social Security Number _____

Address/Zip _____

Phone number _____

Alternate phone number _____

Experience

Name of past employer _____

Dates of employment _____

Phone number of past employer _____

Supervisor's name _____

Job duties _____

Accomplishments _____

Reason for termination _____

Rates of pay _____

Name of past employer _____

Dates of employment _____

Phone number of past employer _____

Supervisor's name _____

Job duties _____

Accomplishments _____

Reason for termination _____

Rates of pay _____

Education

Name of school _____

Dates of attendance _____

Courses taken _____

Grade point average _____

Degree _____

References (get prior permission)

Name _____

Address _____

Phone number _____

Name _____

Address _____

Phone number _____

either complete all parts of the application form or use the terms "will discuss" in sections in which the information presented may appear too negative.

The employer is also looking for the reason for your termination. Were you laid off or were you fired? Is there a problem with your past? Employers want to identify potential problems so that they can avoid employment mistakes. Using the words "will discuss" is a better strategy than simply stating "fired."

Employers also look at the application form to see whether you can work the days and times needed and can meet the physical requirements for the essential functions of the job. This last concern is a legitimate issue for employers, given the new requirements of the Americans with Disabilities Act. (Refer to Chapter 8 for more information on this legislation and how it impacts your job search.)

How do you respond to the question on the application that asks for salary desired? Usually it's best to state "open," unless, of course, you have a definite minimum salary need. It's usually easier to negotiate this issue, since this could be a knock-out question that causes your application form to be rejected if your salary requirements are either too high or too low. If you have been earning at a high salary level, yet are open to earning less because of decreased monetary needs or a desire to enter a new field, it's important to create the opportunity to discuss these issues with the employer.

The Employment Interview

The interview continues to be the most stressful part of the employment process for most of us because it is usually the component of the selection process that must go well for the applicant to get the job. It is one of the leading causes of sweaty palms, dry mouth, and general insecurity that may cause you to reconsider your interest in employment altogether!

Why is the interview so stressful? Probably because it is the fear of the unknown. What will the interviewers ask? What do they want to hear? How can you word your answers to sound positive but not boastful?

One key to a successful interview is reviewing beforehand the questions that will likely be asked in the interview, scripting out appropriate answers, and rehearsing those answers with a friend or family member. Here are some typical questions that may be asked in a selection interview:

+ Tell me a little about yourself.
+ What are you looking for in a job/career?
+ What are your career goals?
+ Tell me about your work history and how it relates to this job.
+ Tell me about your educational background and how it relates to the job.
+ What are your strengths? Weaknesses?
+ Tell me about your last job.

* What are your salary expectations?
* Why did you leave your last job?
* What did you like about your past work experiences?
* Describe the ideal job for you.
* What would your past supervisors say about you?

How to Make the Interview Work

There are any number of ways to keep your interviews on track.

1. *Be prepared.* When you know how to answer questions, it is likely that you will be much more comfortable and will be sure to provide the pertinent job information. By rehearsing your script, you'll improve your chances of saying the right things in the interview. You may find it helpful to read a book on interviewing skills. (Several such books are listed under "Suggested Reading," at the end of the Appendix.)

2. *Establish rapport.* Conversation at the beginning of the interview is a way to establish rapport with the interviewer. This is an important step in the interview process because many jobs are offered to people known to the employer. Take time to connect with the interviewer in a positive way.

One word of caution: We've heard employers say that there are some older adults who carry this point to an extreme and spend too much time chatting, which can create a negative impression. Take the lead from the interviewer and be ready to get down to the business of the interview when signaled, either verbally or nonverbally.

3. *Don't answer questions with a mere yes or no.* Are you answering all questions fully? When we ourselves were inexperienced interviewers, we were always appreciative of those job candidates who would answer questions fully, since we often didn't know how to ask questions in such a way as to get a complete answer. We'd ask questions like, "I see from your résumé that you used to work at XYZ Company," and be horrified when the candidate answered a puzzled, "Yes." Especially in those cases where the person interviewing you

seems inexperienced or untrained, be prepared to provide complete answers that include examples of past performance.

4. *Demonstrate past achievements with examples.* One way in which you can shine in the employment interview is to provide examples of past positive performances. For example, it is much better to say, "I possess leadership skills, and was called on to be the informal group leader whenever my manager was away from the office," than, "I'm a good leader." Behavioral examples—those that demonstrate the context in which actions were taken—are a positive way of showing your qualifications for the job. As an older candidate with years of valuable experience, you can offer some of these examples to employers to demonstrate how your skills and abilities can be attributes on the new job.

5. *Demonstrate a positive attitude.* You will need to be particularly sensitive to the young manager who may already have some reservations about hiring an unretiree and may feel threatened by your maturity and wealth of experience. You should come with the attitude that you have a lot to offer, but are still young enough to learn, grow, and remain flexible.

6. *Keep your strengths in mind.* You may lack self-esteem and confidence and feel uncomfortable in talking about your strengths and abilities. Yet to get the job, you *must* sell yourself in the interview.

7. *Be appropriately dressed.* You should come dressed for the job or even for one level above the job. For an office or clerical position, for instance, you should come dressed for the office manager position. For a plant or industrial job, you should be dressed for the position of plant manager. Be sure to maintain positive body language throughout the interview: shoulders back, head high and a ready smile. Also, be prepared to shake hands with the interviewers—not a fingertip handshake, but a full-hand handshake. Practice with a friend if you're not certain about how to shake hands in the accepted business way.

In her column "Careers," Joyce Lain Kennedy states that the older job seeker should make use of every tool available, such as dress, grooming, speech patterns and mannerisms to project a 1990s viewpoint in the interview. She goes on to say that a positive image doesn't always work, but it certainly works better than a tired, negative attitude.

8. *Be honest.* Nothing will get you eliminated from consideration for a job faster than being dishonest about some aspect of your employment history. Most employers will never consider for employment anyone who has been deceitful in the selection process.

9. *Maintain eye contact.* Ensure that you are making positive eye contact throughout the interview, because many interviewers believe that lack of eye contact with job applicants means dishonesty.

10. *Remember that the selection process is a two-way street.* You are making a selection decision just as much as is the interviewer. Ask good questions to determine if there is a match between you and the job and to show that you are carefully considering the job for which you will be best suited.

11. *Get rid of any negative feelings about past job experiences.* Look at past situations objectively and think about how you will explain them in a positive way to the interviewer. Most everyone has had at least one bad job experience—one in which they were fired, didn't perform up to expectations, or left because of a bad fit. The employer conducting the job interview isn't interested in the particulars of your bad experience. But if, in referring to it, you reveal yourself to be self-pitying, angry, or unforgiving, you may elminate yourself from consideration.

You may feel bitter about a recent employment experience. We've talked with many individuals who have been laid off from their place of employment after years of loyal service and dedication. There are others who have been fired and replaced by the boss's son or daughter. Still others have been forced into early retirement against their wishes.

If you've had a bad job experience, consider how you might share that experience in an honest and positive way with the employer. A friend of ours told us that many years ago she was fired from a job and initially was quite angry about the experience. However, when she began having interviews, she decided she needed to get over her distress and think about how she might present the experience in the most favorable way. Her explanation went something like, "In my past job we had a difference of opinion about how the job should be handled, and so we decided to part ways." Even though she was still pretty bitter over the experience, she didn't share her true feelings ("they made the biggest mistake of their lives") so that she could position herself for the next job opportunity.

Tips for Improving the Interview

Now that we've reviewed reasons why the interview fails, here are some suggestions for improving your next interview:

- Be certain of the time, place, and date, of the interview.
- If you're not sure of the location, do a trial run.
- Arrive early (but not by more than five to ten minutes).
- Take a notepad and a pen; be ready to take notes during the interview.
- Remember the interviewer's name and use it.
- Shake hands—have a firm, full-hand handshake.
- Do not smoke or chew gum during the interview.
- Be polite and respectful to the interviewer.
- Be enthusiastic, upbeat, and positive.
- Tell the truth at all times—but don't tell all!

Selling Yourself in the Interview

As an older adult, you have many attributes to bring to the employment arena. The Job Seekers' Employment Handbook suggests you stress these strengths in the interview:

1. You bring years of experience and training with you.
2. You are less likely to change jobs often.
3. You make the most reliable employee.
4. You are adaptable and eager to learn new things.
5. You will enhance, not threaten, younger employees' work.

6. You are as productive as younger employees at the same skill level.
7. You have fewer family obligations to distract you from your work.
8. You can afford to work for less if the job is more fulfilling.
9. Your health will not negatively affect your work. You are in very good to excellent health to do the job for which you apply. (You should not apply for a job you cannot physically handle.)
10. No one can do the job better than you can![1]

Selling Yourself to Yourself

Before you can sell yourself in an interview, it's imperative that you sell *yourself* on your strengths. Read over the list of your strengths again—and again. Use it as a starting point to make a complete inventory of your strengths and attributes. Tape it to your bathroom mirror and read it over and over until you believe every word of it yourself!

Asking Good Interview Questions

An important part of the interview comes when you are asked if you have any questions. The employer always appreciates well-thought-out questions at this time. Questions that are appropriate to ask during the interview process include:

The Job
- Can you describe what I'll be doing in this job?
- What are the job responsibilities?
- What are the job satisfactions? Dissatisfactions?
- Do you have a job description for this position?
- Can you describe a typical day?
- What will be expected of me?
- How will my performance be judged?

- Why is this position available? Is it due to growth of the company/department?
- Is there something that makes this job particularly difficult?
- Why did the last person leave?
- What will make someone successful in the job?

Training and Development

- What is the company's training and development program?
- How will I be taught the necessary job skills?
- What are the opportunities to learn beyond the immediate job?
- Is the company growing? In what ways?
- What are the career opportunities with this company?
- How have others progressed through the company?
- What are typical career paths?
- What training is provided to support these career paths? What is expected of me in order to move up with the company?

Corporate Philosophy and Culture

- What is the company's philosophy?
- What is the corporate culture?
- What is expected of employees?
- How does the company feel about its employees?
- How does this company contribute to the community?

Questions Not to Ask

Employers appreciate well-thought-out questions from applicants. However, there is one common pet peeve. After a long interview in which the candidate is being seriously considered, he or she is asked, "Do you have any questions that I could answer?" Employers do not appreciate this *initial* response from candidates: "When do I get time off the job?" The question is certainly a legitimate one, but it's inappropriate as the first question directed toward the prospective employer. The applicant hasn't even started the job, and already he or she seems to be asking about time off instead of asking thoughtful questions about the position or the company.

Other questions to avoid at the beginning of the question period include:

- What about my vacation time, sick leave, other time off?
- What can you tell me about the company benefits?
- What can you do for me?

After the Interview

Human resources managers receive thank-you notes from fewer than 10 percent of those individuals interviewed, which makes the practice of writing a thank-you note to those who have interviewed you an excellent way to differentiate yourself from the competition in a positive way. If you are being seriously considered, the thank-you note will reinforce your position.

Since it is such a simple thing to do, make it a part of your job-search process. It doesn't have to be long to be effective. In fact, in three sentences you can complete an effective thank-you. Sentence one should thank the interviewer for his or her time. Sentence two should say why the company should hire you. Sentence three should confirm what you and the interviewer have agreed will be the next step in the process (I'll call you, or you'll call me—whatever was decided).

Write to everyone who gives you a twenty-minute interview or more. Anyone who invested at least twenty minutes in the interviewing process should get a thank-you, since they are probably involved in the decision-making.

Use personal stationery, plain notepaper—anything that looks professional. A handwritten note is just as effective as a typed one. In fact, it may be even more so if it's as neat and legible as possible. If you have awful handwriting, use your typewriter.

Stress the strengths of your background skills that you

brought out in the interview. Highlight the reasons that you should be hired.

Another way to follow up after the interview is to make a telephone call. Here are some tips for following up in a positive way.

1. *Don't be a pest—but be persistent!* I'll never forget one of the women I hired. She had applied, yet was not selected for the job. Nonetheless she kept in touch by making a brief, to-the-point telephone call to me each month. When I finally had another opening, I immediately thought of Suzanne.
2. *Keep your phone calls brief.* Just a few words—"I just wanted to check to see if there were any new openings for which I'm qualified"—are all that's needed.
3. *Show your continued interest.* Let them know you'd like to be a part of the team.
4. *Give a short reminder of your strengths and abilities.*
5. *Ask when to call again.* If a decision hasn't been made, find out when you can call to learn the outcome.
6. *Thank them for their time.*

Finding a job can be the hardest job you'll ever have, but by using some of these effective tools of job search—cover letters, application forms, résumés, and the employment interview—and applying the tips, guidelines, and suggestions offered here, you will be better able to put your experience back to work.

Notes

1. LeeAnn Bernier-Clarke, "Advantages to Hiring a Mature Worker," *Job Seekers' Employment Handbook* (Job Clubs, Inc., 1988).

Chapter 8

Age Discrimination and Ageism: The Dilemmas of Unretirement

Remember, a dead fish can float downstream, but it takes a live one to swim upstream.

—W. C. Fields

In this country, there are laws that protect the employment rights of older adults. The Age Discrimination in Employment Act (ADEA) protects all those forty years of age and older, provided that the employer has twenty or more employees. Further, many states have enacted legislation that equally protects the rights of all individuals, regardless of their age.

Also, the recent passage of the Americans with Disabilities Act (ADA) affords protection to unretirees. It is now considered discrimination if an employer with fifteen or more employees fails to provide the same kinds of employment opportunities for people who are disabled, and for those whom others perceive as being disabled.

Yet many unretirees who strive to keep their jobs or seek new ones are faced with the dilemmas of age discrimination and ageism. What *are* age discrimination and ageism, and what are your rights?

Age Discrimination

Under the requirements of the ADEA, employers may not:

- Fire or refuse to hire you on the basis of age
- Deprive you of employment opportunities because of your age
- Reduce your wage rate because you are older
- Indicate age preference in recruitment advertising

Under the requirements of ADA, employers may not:

- Ask if you have a disability, or if you've ever been disabled
- Request that you take a preemployment medical examination (although preemployment drug testing is permissible)
- Deny you any privilege of employment because of a disability or perception of a disability

Under ADA, employers are also required to "accommodate" those employees or job candidates who can perform the essential functions of the job. This means that it is considered discriminatory if an employer does the following:

- Says that you are too old to handle the job
- Strongly "encourages" you to take retirement
- Fails to hire you because they feel your age would be a detriment
- Asks you, during the preemployment interview, if you have any disabilities, or if you have ever been disabled
- Decreases your salary simply because you are older
- Advertises for young employees by using terms like *recent college graduate, junior executive,* and *young, energetic*
- Fails to place you in a certain position because of fears that you might hurt yourself or that you might not be physically able to do the job
- Passes you over for special training, professional development, or educational opportunities
- Fails to promote you on the basis of age

♦ Will not place you in certain positions because of real or perceived customer preferences

Ageism

Ageism is a much more subtle form of discrimination in an organization. Much like racism and sexism, its actions may not be illegal or discriminatory in the legal sense, but ageist actions often have the effect of closing employment doors for older adults.

Ageism can take the following forms:

♦ Using language that is offensive to older adults, such as "old codger," "old coot," or "old buzzard"
♦ Failing to provide older adults with the tools for success on the job
♦ Phasing older adults out of important job duties
♦ Omitting older adults from meetings, correspondence, or other channels of communication
♦ Expressing negative attitudes about old age
♦ Revealing stereotypical thinking about what older adults can and can't do
♦ Treating older adults in a disrespectful manner (when younger employees are treated with greater deference)

Avoiding Age Discrimination

While many organizations are seeing the value of unretirees, there are many managers, supervisors, and co-workers who may openly fight your employment in a discriminatory manner, or may subtly make your employment difficult.

What should you do to avoid age discrimination in your unretirement? Outlined here are some ideas for minimizing discrimination and ageism.

Planning Your Job Search

1. *Focus on those employers who already recognize the value of hiring experienced, mature workers.* Examine the compa-

nies mentioned in Chapter 1 that have demonstrated an interest in hiring unretirees, for instance.

2. *Attend job and career fairs for older adults.* Make note of the companies participating in the fair, and apply there. These organizations have already recognized the value of maturity.

3. *Focus on small, growing companies.* These are the ones that can benefit the most from your varied background and wealth of experience. They also tend to be the companies with the most positions available.

4. *Apply at those companies whose customers are older adults.* These organizations can readily benefit from your inside customer knowledge.

5. *Indicate your interest in working part-time hours or temporary assignments.* Many organizations have difficulty in filling these positions with reliable, mature employees who genuinely care about their work.

During Your Job Search

1. *Omit any references to age on your résumé, and omit age information on the application form.* Be sure to indicate that you are over eighteen years old if that information is requested. Note: Do not falsify information on your application or résumé; this is generally grounds for termination/disqualification. Also, you will be required, once you land the job, to provide birth date and other legitimate information for processing your benefits.

2. *Omit any indirect references to age on your résumé.* For example, if you've worked for an organization for a long period of time, you will probably want to omit the dates of employment, since these will provide clues to the employer as to your age. Also, some older adults with many years of experience with an organization or an industry are stating that they have ten-plus years of experience instead of indicating that they have worked twenty-five years for an employer.

3. *Include recent dates that add to your credibility.* For example, if you just returned to school to receive a certificate

or degree, be sure to include those dates prominently on your résumé.

4. *Is it important for the employer to know about your first job out of high school or college?* If that job just isn't relevant or important, leave it out. In fact, you may want to include revelant job information, for example, only for the past ten years.

5. *Don't focus on your age in the interview.* Of course, you *can* if the interviewer has clearly indicated that your age is an asset.

6. *Avoid references to your retirement, if, in fact, you have retired.* This may make some employers nervous about your longevity on the job, or may make them question your interest in employment.

7. *Focus on your recent accomplishments.* Be sure to mention any recent training, activities, interests, and specific job-related experience during the interview.

8. *Don't talk negatively about young people.* Don't indicate any discomfort in working with younger co-workers or managers.

9. *Be sure to address the concerns of the interviewer.* Respond appropriately to ageist or discriminatory questions (refer to the listing in this chapter).

Once You've Landed the Job

1. *Don't focus on your age.* Instead, focus on your abilities and your strengths. Show how your age can be an asset through your maturity, experience, and judgment without making it the focal point of discussions.

2. *Accept opportunities for training, professional development, and educational opportunities whenever possible.* You won't be considered qualified to continue in your job or be considered for promotion if you don't have the knowledge and skills to progress.

3. *Don't talk about retirement.* It's hard for employers to think of you as a key player if you keep talking about your retirement from the organization. Bring up the

issue of retirement only when you are sure that you are ready.

4. *Provide support for other individuals in the organization.* Many unretirees serve as role models and mentors for younger co-workers. By playing this role in an organization, you add value.

5. *Understand how your performance is judged in the organization.* What are the performance guidelines and standards? Do you know how you rate? Document your performance if possible.

Knowing Your Rights

You may be wondering about a specific situation in which you were the target of ageist or discriminatory practices. We are frequently asked questions about how unretirees should deal with discrimination in the workplace. Outlined here are some suggestions for dealing with specific issues of age discrimination and ageism:

I believe I've been discriminated against by my employer. Should I sue?

Even when you know that you have been discriminated against because of your age, there are a number of points to consider before you file a charge. First, an age discrimination suit takes a great deal of time and energy and also takes a toll on one's positive mind-set. While there are good reasons for bringing suits (such as creating awareness in the employer and bringing about changes in the workplace), the question is: Is it worth it? Could your time be better spent in finding another job? Would you be consumed with bitterness? Is it for you? Only you can answer these questions.

What if I hear (or believe) that I was not hired because of my age?

You have the right to file a charge of discrimination if you believe that you were not hired because of your age. However, as a first step you might want to talk with the employer before filing a claim. The employer may be very eager to avoid a charge of discrimination, and may be happy to talk with you about the company's decision. Or you can simply file a charge with the Equal Employment Opportunity Commission or with your local/state human rights commission.

Is an offer of early retirement discriminatory?

Offers of early retirement can be either discriminatory or nondiscriminatory, depending on how the employer goes about making the offer to employees. Offers of early retirement that are voluntary and noncoercive are generally legitimate.

The lines may seem blurry at best, however, when you are trying to determine whether or not an organization has offered retirement as a genuinely voluntary option. What if your boss hounds you about whether or not you'll be retiring? What if you believe that your job may go away if you don't accept an offer of early retirement? A Senate report states that retirement is forced, and therefore discriminatory, when "a reasonable person would have concluded there was no choice but to accept the offer."

What if I am asked to waive my rights to sue when I take early retirement from my employer?

Increasingly, employers are asking employees who accept early retirement to sign a release that waives the individual's rights to sue under ADEA. These releases are acceptable if the exiting employee signs them voluntarily and if the benefits received are not in exchange for benefits to which the employee is already entitled.

The employer has the following additional obligations:[1]

- The release language should be clear and understandable.
- The release should be fully explained to the individual.
- The employee should be encouraged to seek his or her own legal counsel.
- The employee should have sufficient time to review the release.

- Damages should be outlined in the event the individual files a discrimination claim.

Responding to Discriminatory Questions Relating to Age

Many employers today do not understand what they may legitimately ask in an employment interview. Others may simply be unaccustomed to interviewing older applicants and not know where to begin. We discovered one cartoon in which an older woman is being asked by her interviewer, "I see from your résumé that you used to be younger. What made you change?"

At Kentucky Fried Chicken, there were many managers who had traditionally hired young people to fill open positions and who were at a loss as to what questions to ask of older candidates. They had historically asked such questions as, "What was your first job after high school?" "What is your favorite high school class?" and "How will you juggle work, homework, and school activities?" These managers were stumped when confronted by an older job seeker.

While employers may ask you questions about your age, they may not use this information in a discriminatory manner. Therefore, while asking an age-related question is not illegal per se, the courts have generally found that asking this type of question is a sign of age discrimination (and some states have legislation that makes these preemployment inquiries illegal).

Similarly, employers may ask *indirect* questions that could reveal age; however, these, too, are generally interpreted as being discriminatory. A cartoon in one of the American Association of Retired Persons' publications depicted a personnel manager saying to an older job applicant, "Your age means nothing to us. All we want to know is your college graduation date." This is an employer who would have some serious answering to do if faced with a claim of age discrimination.

What do you do, then, if faced with an inappropriate question relating to age? Below, we've outlined possible responses to some of the common inappropriate questions relating to age. Not all these answers are appropriate in every situation, however. In fact, some of the answers would need to be delivered with a smile, or certainly with a sense of humor to not be construed as flip or hostile.

Perhaps the best answers to each of these inappropriate employer questions are, "Why do you ask?" and "What are your concerns?" These responses attempt to determine what is at the heart of the question so that an appropriate response can be offered.

You may want to study this list and adapt one or two responses to your own situation and personality.

How Old Are You?

- I'm old enough to offer maturity, experience, and judgment, and I'm young enough to learn, grow, and change.
- I'm old enough to drink.
- I'm old enough to know better.
- I'm old enough to do this job.
- In dog years, I'm less than ten years old.
- Why do you ask?
- I'm older than you are!
- I'm old enough to vote.
- I'm the perfect age—aged to perfection!
- What age do you think I am?
- What age would you like me to be?
- I'm old enough to sleep by myself, and young enough to worry about it.
- I'm young enough to do the job, and old enough to do it right.
- There are two things I vowed never to do: tell my age and tell my bosses' secrets.
- Chronologically I'm _____ years old, but mentally and physically I'm about forty!
- I consider myself to be a seasoned, experienced worker.
- I don't plan to collect Social Security.
- I plan to work for a long time.
- What are your concerns?
- I already have health benefits.

- I hope you're around as long as I!
- I'm old enough to have seen changes in this industry . . . the best, the worst, and how to deal with them.
- I'm _____ years old and ready to give you ten good years.
- I'm glad you asked. I'm old enough to provide you with the work ethic you need.
- I'm young enough to have a mortgage and old enough to need financial planning.
- I'm old enough to have seen your company grow, and I want to be a part of it.
- I'm young enough to look forward to Social Security . . . someday.
- Between eighteen and death.

When Were You Born?

- I don't think the year is as important as my level of experience.
- Why do you ask?
- What are your concerns?
- Long after George Washington was president.
- When do you think?

Aren't You Overqualified?

- Why do you ask?
- That depends on what kind of experience you're talking about.
- You can never know too much.
- Wouldn't you prefer someone who was overqualified to one who was underqualified?
- What are your concerns?

Can You Handle the Physical Demands of This Job?

- I walk two miles every morning.
- Why do you ask?
- There's no moss growing here.
- Here's what I can do. . . .
- What are the physical demands of the job?

- I haven't missed a day of work in five years.
- What are your concerns?

How Is Your Health?

- My health is fine. Just ask my boyfriend/girlfriend!
- Why do you ask?
- I've been around long enough to be immune.
- I'm better than ever!
- I exercise, walk, and hike.
- I haven't missed a day of work in five years.
- I have a twenty-three-year-old wife and a three-year-old son.
- I taught Jack Palance how to do one-arm push-ups.
- Nothing prevents me from doing my job.
- What concerns do you have?
- My health is fine. Thanks for asking!
- I'm slowing down. It now takes me four and a half minutes to run a four-minute mile.
- I'm feeling great . . . and you?
- I wish I'd felt this good at twenty!
- I'm getting better and younger every day.
- I have no health problems to keep me from doing this job.
- My health is in better shape than my wealth.

How Do You Feel About Working for a Younger Manager?

- Great!
- My children have been managing me for years.
- I work well with people of all ages.
- You're never too old or too young to start learning.
- Why do you ask?
- What are your concerns?
- It depends on how cute he/she is.
- I love working with kids.

When Did You Graduate From High School?

- What are your concerns?
- I graduated the year I was supposed to.

- I graduated when a high school diploma meant something.
- It was a year that will go down in history.
- June.
- Is this a requirement for the job?
- I did graduate from high school.
- Just a short while ago.
- Why do you ask?
- I just got my GED.
- It seems like only yesterday.
- I'd tell you, but then you'd know I'm over twenty-one!
- It was a beautiful spring night.
- I can't remember.
- Before college.
- After my senior year.
- I'm ready to go back to work!
- Do you want to know about the curriculum?
- I went to school when classical education was the norm.
- I have a good quality education that can be put to good use for you.
- I graduated and got my first job when the work ethic was very important.
- Quite a few years ago, but let me tell you about my recent training.

Do You Have a Disability?

- Not unless gray hair is a disability.
- I have many . . . but I can do the job.
- No.
- What are your concerns?
- I have *cap*abilities.
- Do you need one for Affirmative Action purposes?
- Why do you ask?
- What are the essential job functions for this job?

What Are Your Children's Ages?

- I won't be getting any calls from school.
- What are your concerns?

- My children pay for their own baby-sitters.
- Why do you ask?

What Are Your Goals?

- I want to be _____ when I grow up.
- I want to supplement my income.
- I want to enlarge my skill base.
- I want to be with people.
- I want to share the benefit of my experience with your company.
- I want to be productive.
- I want to make my first million.
- I want to stay in the workforce for a career opportunity.
- I want to get away from my retired spouse and adult children!
- Why do you ask?
- What concerns do you have?

Won't Working Jeopardize Your Social Security Benefits?

- Yes, but I'm not interested!
- Social Security may not be around when I'm really ready to retire.
- Yes, but I want to supplement my income.
- I'm looking for a part-time schedule to meet our mutual needs.
- My kids get it, but I've never looked into it.
- I'm not eligible yet.
- I can earn up to $_____ without jeopardizing my benefits.
- I'm more interested in working.

Notes

1. David Israel and Stephen P. Beiser, "Are Age Discrimination Releases Enforceable?" *HRMagazine*, August 1990, pp. 80–81.

Chapter 9

Le Troisième Âge: A Time for Training and Retraining

First say to yourself what you would be; and then do what you have to do.

—Epictetus, Greek philosopher

"Le Troisième Âge" is the French term for the Third Age—or the period of life following the First Age of growing up and the Second Age of working and parenting. Charles Handy, in an article featured in *Modern Maturity* magazine, states, "It can be a time for a new style of living and working and earning that no one could or should call 'retirement.' "[1]

New Life Patterns: The Cyclic Life

Ken Dychtwald, coauthor of *Age Wave*, states that, given the longer, healthier lives of adults today, the notion of a linear approach to life, with education first, work second, and leisure third, is unrealistic. "Longer life will eliminate the rigid correlations between age and the various activities and challenges of adult life," he states. In his view, a cyclic approach, in which we will combine education, work, and leisure in new ways *throughout* our lifetimes will become the norm.[2]

The Importance of Lifelong Learning

If you are going to achieve your goals in unretirement, it will probably be necessary to make a commitment to lifelong learning. Training and retraining can help you in the following ways:

1. *To stay current in your job.* Technology is changing, and so are the careers that it supports. To stay active in your field, you'll need to receive new skills training, education, and retraining to keep pace with the changes taking place. Employees at Bank of America, for example, found that they needed to participate in the organization's retraining efforts in order to maintain their employment. The organization was forced to eliminate 15,000 jobs in 300 branch offices, and accomplished this through attrition. Those left behind had to learn new roles.[3]

2. *To avoid career burnout.* More and more executives are facing emotional and physical exhaustion on the job and finding that these can be alleviated through job redesign, cross-training, stress management, and sabbatical leaves, states AARP in a brochure for employers titled *How to Train Older Workers*.

3. *To avoid career plateauing.* For managers and other professionals in positions with no opportunity for advancement, AARP suggests that training and development opportunities may be one strategy to assist individuals. This is true whether your unretirement decision is to stay in your current job or to move on to another job or another field.

4. *To avoid career obsolescence.* Internal retraining courses, career planning workshops, educational assistance programs, and involvement in professional organizations are all ways of staying current.[4]

5. *To get a new job or enter a new field.* Many new jobs require certification, licensure, or updated classes in new technology and methods.

Employer Fears About Unretirees and Training/Retraining

Unfortunately, the old adage "You can't teach an old dog new tricks" is still alive and well today. Many people believe that it's difficult if not impossible to train or retrain unretirees. Just examine these facts highlighting employer fears about training and older adults:

- According to a study conducted by AARP, only three out of ten employers currently include older adults in their training activities, even when they do not have mandatory retirement policies.
- In a study conducted by the Society for Human Resource Management (SHRM), 59 percent of employers believed that older adults show resistance to training.
- The same SHRM study revealed that 52 percent of employers believe that older adults have difficulties in training.[5]

Given these negative perceptions on the part of employers, it is important to also analyze the facts about how training may be different for you than for your younger counterparts.

- Unretirees can take up to two times as long to learn. Not everyone learns at the same speed, and some older adults are definitely slower to learn new pieces of information.
- How we perceive light changes as we grow older. Older eyes find it more difficult to see high-gloss materials, and may not see some pastel colors as clearly.
- We may not hear or see as clearly as we grow older. Vision and hearing can deteriorate as the aging process occurs, making small print and soft, high-pitched sounds more challenging.
- It may take us longer to store and retrieve data as we grow older. However, mental functioning is seldom affected until age seventy or later.
- Older adults are less familiar with high technology than their younger counterparts. Often, the unretiree has had less exposure to computers and high-tech equipment than younger workers have had.[6] In a survey commissioned by the Markle Foundation, only 9 percent of people ages sixty to sixty-nine own computers, and only

3 percent over the age of seventy; in comparison, about 20 percent of all American households own computers.[7]

How You Learn and How You Can Maximize Your Learning

Adults of all ages learn according to a set of learning principles acknowledged by educators and trainers. These principles are briefly described below. For each principle, we've listed ways in which you can maximize your own learning.[8]

The Law of Effect

We learn best when we are in pleasant, comfortable surroundings in which we feel that it's all right to make a mistake. To maximize your learning:

- Whenever possible, choose a classroom situation in which you feel comfortable.
- If you don't find that your employer offers you the kind of learning environment you prefer, seek other ways to provide for your education. For example, one unretiree decided to enroll in a special computer club especially for older adults when she found that her employer's course was too uncomfortable. (She was with primarily younger co-workers who had had lots of computer experience.)
- Request special tutoring if you need assistance.

The Law of Exercise

We all learn best when we can try out and practice what we have learned. After hearing a lecture, for example, it's helpful to actually try out what you've learned. Simulations, role-plays, and other activities help reinforce what's been learned. To maximize your learning:

- Get actively involved in your learning. Don't sit back and expect to be spoon-fed. You'll learn best when you become a part of the training.

- Volunteer for role-plays and other class exercises. These will reinforce your learning.
- Take information home to study. Practice makes perfect.
- Put training ideas into action as soon as practical.

The Law of Readiness

We all learn best when we're motivated to learn. When we understand how we can apply a piece of information, we're more motivated to make it ours. To gain the most from training:

- Ask why, and find out the application for the training. Once you know how you'll use the training, you'll be more inclined to learn.
- Find out what the rewards will be for completing the training. In many organizations, pay increases and promotions are linked to the achievement of training and retraining goals.

The Law of Association

We learn best when we add what we learn to what we've learned in past experiences, building-block style. To gain the most from training:

- Consider how a new piece of information, a skill, or any learning objective is similar to something with which you are already familiar.
- Use analogies to enhance learning points.
- Brush up on the basics so that you'll be ready for the next step in the training.

The Law of Primacy

We all learn best what we learn first. To maximize your learning:

- Take a break when you can from learning. A brief stretch period will permit you to return to the training ready for the next learning point.

- Revisit the basics so that you can build upon your past learning.

Where to Find Training and Retraining Opportunities

Training and retraining opportunities are literally everywhere, and specialized educational programming for older adults is becoming increasingly popular. Outlined here are some resources to help you explore the training and development opportunities that are right for your needs today.

Look to Your Employer for Training and Retraining

Northwestern National Life Insurance Co. hires unretirees to staff its claims center in Tucson, Arizona, and provides tailored training for the part-time claims processors and customer service representatives. Because they have focused on targeted recruitment efforts aimed at unretirees, they find that they can tailor their training to the specific needs of older adults.[9]

General Electric Co.'s Aerospace Electronic Systems in Utica, New York, switched from analog to digital technology in the 1970s, and found that retraining their own employees provided them with a 3-to-1 cost savings ratio and permitted them to retain their experienced staff. Harris Trust & Savings Bank offers eighty ongoing training programs for its employees, many of whom are retirees who assist in peak periods on a part-time basis. McMasters, a special employment and training initiative offered by McDonald's, provides on-the-job training in its popular program. General Dynamics Corp. in San Diego, California, offers retraining for all of its employees who must be kept up-to-date on the newest technology.[10]

Your employer may also assist you in earning your General Education Development (GED) certificate if you haven't yet received your high school diploma. Or you can contact your local public school system for information on free evening classes or at-home courses to prepare for the examination.

Investigate College and Vocational School Programs

You can complete your undergraduate degree, get a master's, or obtain a new and different degree. Community colleges like Dundalk Community College in Maryland encourage unretirees to take courses on campus by offering tuition waivers, precampus counseling, and remedial supports. One special service offered is a full semester of orientation, in which participants visit each department, meet faculty, and spend time in the labs. Many of the courses offered are geared to older students.[11]

Many college and university programs, such as Harvard's Institute for Learning in Retirement and Eckard College's Academy of Senior Professionals, are targeted to the older adult. Harvard's program has older adults as both students and professors and enrolls some 400 students each semester for a fraction of the normal tuition. Eckard involves more than 120 unretirees as advisors, career counselors, and mentors to students.[12] Other colleges permit unretirees to attend regular college classes without paying tuition.

ElderHostel is an international educational program offering one-week courses in colleges in the United States, Canada, Great Britain, and Scandinavia. Based in Boston, this nonprofit program permits unretirees to live in dormitories, eat in campus dining halls, and study courses as diverse as music, history, and astronomy.

Explore Government-Funded Employment and Training Programs

There are a number of government-funded employment and training programs providing services to unretirees. Both the Job Training Partnership Act (JTPA) and the Senior Community Services Employment Program (SCSEP) offer training for income-eligible individuals over the age of fifty-five. JTPA programs operate through local public/private partnerships, called Private Industry Councils (PICs). The SCSEP operates through ten national sponsors and through nonprofit agencies across the country. The ten national sponsors include:

1. American Association of Retired Persons
2. Green Thumb
3. National Association for Hispanic Elderly
4. National Caucus and Center on Black Aged
5. National Council of Senior Citizens
6. National Council on the Aging
7. National Forest Service
8. National Indian Council on Aging, Inc.
9. National Pacific/Asian Resource Center on Aging
10. National Urban League

Refer to the resource guide in the Appendix for contact information on each of the national sponsor headquarters, and for state JTPA contact information.

You may also be eligible for two additional government-funded or -sponsored training programs. The first is the dislocated worker program, offered to individuals who have been laid off by their employers and operated through funding provided by JTPA. The second is the displaced homemaker program, available to women who must return to the workplace as a result of the death of a spouse or a divorce. (Consult the Appendix for additional contact information.)

Check Out Special Classes and Programs for Unretirees

There are a number of unique programs being offered across the country for training and retraining for unretirees. Be on the lookout for similar programs being offered in your community.

♦ *SeniorNet* is a nonprofit organization at the University of San Francisco that runs twenty-eight computer centers across the United States and Canada exclusively for those fifty-five years of age and older. The organization offers special classes in computer software, as well as providing a telecommunications network so that participants can communicate via computer and modem to other participants across the country. There is a nominal membership fee

♦ *Silver Fox Computer Club* in Louisville, Kentucky, is a division of Business Computers and Software and offers unretirees the opportunity to learn computer software skills alongside other older adults. There is a yearly membership fee of $50, which permits members to participate in any one of the courses being offered each month. They can also take additional courses for $10 per class.

At Silver Fox, all the instructors are over fifty. Individuals wanting to update their computer skills join, as do corporations wishing to provide tailored training for older employees. Some members, like Dr. Richard Gibson, use the course to help them in their businesses. Dr. Gibson, a dentist, has attended Silver Fox to learn how to computerize his dental office records.[13]

♦ *Senior Center in the Schools* is a pilot intergenerational program initiated at Pleasure Ridge Park High School in Louisville, Kentucky. The center advertises that "It's never too late to go back to school," in their flyers distributed to area unretirees. The center permits unretirees to participate in school programs and projects with students, and provides services such as eye screenings, counseling, Social Security and Medicare information. It also provides lunches five days a week. Participants can volunteer as library aides, tutors, teachers' aides, guest speakers, and office aides. The program is offered as a cooperative effort of the county government, the local school system, and the U.S. Department of Health and Human Services.

♦ *Cruise lines* are also getting into the educational picture by offering special workshops and lectures on such varied subjects as money management, writing skills, and computer software applications. Royal Cruise Lines, for example, provides the opportunity for its passengers to attend sessions focused on financial advice, retirement planning, and computer programming.[14]

Action Strategies

Here are some training-and-development action strategies to consider as you create your unretirement plan.

♦ Before beginning any training or retraining program, be sure that whatever education you pursue leads you to the unretirement option you want. There are some free college courses, Elderhostel courses, and other programs that are fun, but are not vocationally oriented, or that may not lead you to the career path you want. And remember that training is not an automatic admission to the unretirement option of your dreams.

♦ Talk to your supervisor or human resources professional (if you're currently working) to determine what training and retraining options might be available. Perhaps your employer offers in-house educational programs or makes available on-going college or professional development courses through a tuition program. Take advantage of the benefits you already have.

♦ Develop a sense of adventure. Try something you've always wanted to do but never had the time or opportunity to pursue. Perhaps your hobby or long-term interest can be turned into a business or a new job.

♦ Keep an open mind and be open to new experiences. Be willing to reconsider past ideas about what you might do.

♦ Be positive and be willing to give it a try. Unretirees who think they are too old to learn usually are; it's a self-fulfilling prophesy.

Unretirement can offer you the opportunity to obtain new skills, abilities, and knowledge that will help you realize your dreams. By taking advantage of employer-sponsored education, by taking a college course or completing a degree, by enrolling in a special learning program for older adults, or by exploring a new educational concept, you can gain the tools to remain updated in your field and stay competitive in today's job market.

Notes

1. Charles Handy, "Building Smaller Fires," *Modern Maturity*, October–November 1991, p. 35.

2. Ken Dychtwald and Joe Flower, *Age Wave* (Los Angeles: Tarcher, 1989), p. 95.
3. David V. Lewis, "Make Way for the Older Worker," *HRMagazine*, May 1990, p. 76.
4. Catherine D. Fyock, *America's Work Force Is Coming of Age: What Every Business Needs to Know to Recruit, Train, Manage, and Retain an Aging Work Force* (Lexington, Mass.: Lexington Books/Macmillan, 1990), pp. 115–116.
5. Carol Kleiman, "Firms Find That, with Retraining, Older Is Better, *Chicago Tribune*, February 4, 1990, 8–1.
6. Fyock, *America's Work Force*, pp. 104–105.
7. "A New—and Older—Generation Begins Computing," *Indianapolis Star*, April 25, 1990, B7.
8. Fyock, *America's Work Force*, pp. 102–103.
9. Dave Shadovitz, "Training Report," *Human Resource Executive*, June, p. 23.
10. Kleiman, "Firms Find."
11. Donald E. Gelfand, *The Aging Network: Programs and Services*, 3d ed. (New York: Springer Publishing, 1988), p. 130.
12. Dychtwald, *Age Wave*, p. 149.
13. Elaine Thomas, "Computer Club's Success Shows How Strategy Works," *Business First*, February 1991, p. 33.
14. Dychtwald, *Age Wave*, p. 153.

Chapter 10

The Road to Unretirement

Giving up is the ultmate tragedy.

—Robert J. Donovan

The road to unretirement can be an exciting one, one that will lead you to realize your dreams in finding or keeping the kind of work that meets your needs. In this chapter we're going to help you get on the road to unretirement by examining the barriers that may still exist on that road, and helping you overcome those obstacles to your success. We'll also explore how other unretirees just like you have found happiness along the unretirement trail.

Attitudinal Barriers

We received a phone call after an article had appeared in the local paper regarding our work with older workers. The woman said that she wanted assistance in finding a job, but as the conversation developed, she whined, complained, and repeatedly said, "I can't do that," "That won't work for me," "I'm too old," and other self-defeating remarks.

In working with career counselors who provide job-search assistance to older job seekers, we often hear that these older individuals can be their own worst enemy in finding happiness in unretirement. In a series of workshops we have collected the most-often-heard phrases that are a barrier to employment. We have listed these self-defeating statements below, together with ways to help you rethink your position if you catch yourself in this negative-thinking trap.

1. *"No one hires people my age."* But they do! Just look at the many examples we've offered in this book! Work with a placement counselor or job-search professional to get in touch with others who have found the unretirement option that was right for them. Join a job club for older adults, or work for a temporary help agency that specializes in placing older adults.

If you do get caught in this thinking trap, one suggestion is to consider how *young* you are, not how old you are. Consider your strengths, your abilities, and your skills. (Refer to Chapter 5 if you want to reassess yourself.) Review what employers are looking for, and think about what you have to offer. And remember, while there may be some employers (or some individuals) who think you're too old, you just need to find those who see the benefits of hiring someone with your experience.

2. *"I don't want to/can't work full-time."* You don't have to. As we've outlined in Chapters 3 and 4, there are many part-time, temporary, and other flexible scheduling arrangements that can help you arrange the kind of workday, workweek, work month, or work year that appeals to you. There may also be appropriate work opportunities through placement with a temporary help agency.

If you find yourself making this statement, you need to ask yourself if you are really just making an excuse for not seeking work. Do you really want to work? The choice is yours.

3. *"Employers don't want people like me."* Employers want to hire employees who can help them meet their needs. If you can be at work on time every day, if you can work with enthusiasm and energy, if you can offer superior service to customers, if you understand the value of quality work, then you are someone who is desired by employers.

You may be using this statement if you have been unfortunate and come into contact with an employer who has fears about hiring an older adult. Managers may be threatened by hiring someone older than they. Seek out the many employers who see the value in hiring employees with experience and judgment, and who want to put your experience back to work.

4. *"There are no jobs available that I want."* There are many jobs that offer the kind of challenges, flexibility, and opportu-

nities you may be seeking. Often the problem boils down to the fact that *finding* a job is one of the most difficult jobs anyone ever undertakes. If you are serious about unretirement, you will need to become serious about your job search. Most job-search professionals say that to be successful in finding the opportunity that is right for you, you will need to spend about thirty-five hours each week working on your search. Also, for those of you with greater salary requirements, it will take longer to find the right job.

Outplacement professionals indicate that a rule of thumb for a managerial, professional, or executive level job search is about one month per $10,000 of income expected. Therefore, if your salary expectations are in the $50,000 range, you can expect to spend about five months on your job search.

5. *"I'll lose flexibility and spontaneity in my life."* There is no doubt that working reduces your ability to remain totally flexible and spontaneous about planning travel, spending time with grandchildren, and meeting other needs and responsibilities. However, having a job does not mean that you'll need to relinquish all flexibility.

As we discussed in Chapters 3 and 4, you may find opportunities to remain flexible with the variety of alternative scheduling arrangements that are becoming popular. Job sharing, flex-scheduling, part-time, and telecommuting may offer you the kind of schedule that will give you the flexibility you want and need.

6. *"I want to do some fun things (spend time with grandchildren, travel, work with hobbies) that I can't do if I work."* There are a variety of work schedules that can give you the time (and often the funds) to do the enjoyable things you want to do. Are you using this statement as an excuse for not working? What are your real priorities?

7. *"My children don't want me to work."* In many cases, children have expectations that their parents will take the easy road and retire when they reach age sixty-five. It may be that your adult children dream of playing golf, fishing, or pursuing travel or other hobbies themselves. They may even think that Mom and Dad are too old to work.

One counselor told us that she often heard this remark

from unretirees, and began asking them, "Do your children always do what you want them to do?" and "Are your children willing to provide you with the funds you want and need throughout your retirement?" or "Whose life is it, anyway?"

8. *"I'll be embarrassed if others find out I'm working."* Some individuals feel that, since retirement has recently been seen as the American dream, their friends will think that they are working because they've mismanaged their money, because they are destitute, or because they have failed in some way.

Are you using other people's yardstick to measure your own success? What is it that you want? If working meets your financial, professional, social, or spiritual goals, why do you care what others think? Go for the goals that are important to you.

You Can Do It!

You can do whatever you want to do. It's a matter of having the right attitude about unretirement. In the book *Aging Well*, by James F. Fries, M.D. (Reading, Mass.: Addison-Wesley, 1989), the paradox of aging and capacity is discussed. He states that while our capacity diminishes as we grow older, we can still improve in many areas because we never reach our full potential. When it comes to learning a new skill as an older adult, our capacity to learn and perform may be less than it would have been when we were young, but there is still plenty of room for growth and development, since few of us realize our potential.

While many older adults feel that they have to give up because they can't be the *best* at some skill or ability, it is encouraging to realize that we can always learn a new task or activity, and, given practice, go on improving at it.

Slowing Down the Aging Process

Gerontologists agree that many of the manifestations of aging can be slowed down or reversed with lifestyle changes and adaptations. James Fries also offers suggestions for helping slow down the aging process. He identifies these steps:

1. Maintain independence.
2. Moderate your habits.
3. Keep active.
4. Be enthusiastic.
5. Have pride.
6. Be individual.[1]

Be a Quester

In her book *Dare to Change Your Job—And Your Life* (New York: Master Media, 1987), Carole Kanchier uses the term *questers* to describe those who are ready for occupational changes and have prepared themselves to move into new occupations or activities. She states that anyone interested in pursuing a satisfying career should take on the attributes of a quester and become more flexible, open-minded, adaptable, and inner-directed.

Using Positive Talk

Having a positive spirit can also mean avoiding phrases that may be construed as negative or stereotypical. In their book *Finding the Right Job at Midlife*, Jeffrey G. Allen and Jess Gorkin list phrases that should be avoided by older adults:

- "At my age . . ."
- "Back in the days when . . ."
- "Back then . . ."
- "I can't . . ."
- "In the (good) old days . . ."
- "It used to be that . . ."
- "I remember when . . ."
- "Listen, son . . ."
- "Nowadays . . ."

- "Old-timers like me . . ."
- ". . . over the hill"
- "Physical exertion . . ."
- "The girls in the office . . ."
- ". . . up in years"
- "Way back when . . ."
- "We used to . . ."
- "When I was younger . . ."
- "When I was your age . . ."
- "When you get to be my age . . ."
- "Years ago . . ."[2]

Watch the expressions you use, and avoid those that put you or others in a negative frame of mind about your abilities as an unretiree.

Aging = Living

Consider your attitude toward aging. Do you think aging is about growing closer to death, or do you regard aging as the opportunity to live a longer life? How old is "old" to you? Do you see your life as half over, or half yet to be lived? The choice is yours.

How you perceive aging will also affect how others perceive your age. We've heard successful unretirees tell us that once they forget about their age, others do too.

You've heard the expression "You're as old as you feel." How old do you choose to feel? You can be old at forty, or young at eighty. It's up to you.

We like the attitude toward aging and living displayed in this poem by Ruth Harriet Jacobs, from her book *Be an Outrageous Older Woman* (Glen Rock, N.J.: Knowledge, Ideas & Trends, Inc., 1991).

Don't Call Me a Young Woman

Don't call me a young woman;
it's not a compliment or courtesy
but rather a grating discourtesy.

Being old is a hard won achievement
not something to be brushed aside
treated as infirmity or ugliness
or apologized away by "young woman."
I'm an old woman, a long liver.
I'm proud of it. I revel in it.
I wear my grey hair and wrinkles
as badges of triumphant survival
and I intend to grow even older.

Don't call me a young woman.
I was a young woman for years
but that was then and this is now.
I was a mid life woman for a time
and I celebrated that good span.
Now, I am somebody magnificent, new
a seer, wise woman, old proud crone,
an example and mentor to the young
who need to learn old women wisdom.
I look back on jobs well done
and learn to do different tasks now.
I think great thoughts and share them.

Don't call me a young woman.
You reveal your own fears of aging.
Maybe you'd better come learn from
all of us wonderful old women
how to take the sum of your life
with all its experience and knowledge
and show how a fully developed life
can know the job of a past well done
and the job of life left to live.

                                        —Ruth Harriet Jacobs

What Makes Unretirees Successful?

In several studies funded by the AARP Andrus Foundation, the motivations for older workers were analyzed, along with the reasons that some unretirees stayed on the job. In the first study, conducted by Dr. E. Michael Brady at the University of Southern Maine, 200 newly hired older workers were interviewed to determine their reasons for working or seeking employment.

The most common reasons cited were the desire to feel useful, the desire for extra income, the desire to meet people, the need for a challenge, and the wish to do something different from what they had done in their preretirement life. While money was still a consideration in seeking employment, more important were intrinsic benefits—"psychic income"—such as a sense of accomplishment, friendly co-workers, and interesting work.

What kept the workers on the job? In a follow-up interview, 75 percent of those contacted were still with their employers because they enjoyed having responsibility for making decisions, the opportunity to use their skills, and the ability to work without close supervision. Employers valued their unretirees because of their reliability, experience, work ethic, attention to detail, fewer absences, enthusiasm for their work, and general excellence as employees.[3]

Success Stories

Stories abound of unretirees who are realizing their dreams. Famous individuals like Colonel Harland D. Sanders are among them. Did you know that the Colonel began Kentucky Fried Chicken when most people might have been content to sit back and settle for their first Social Security check? He owned a gas station in which he served his famous secret-recipe fried chicken to folks traveling the state highway. When the interstate highway was built, it rerouted all that traffic away from his station. Instead of throwing in the towel, he decided to go for his dream. He began to prepare his chicken recipe for other restaurant owners and offered to make these owners franchisees. Of course those who accepted his handshake offer are millionaires today. The Colonel was able to turn a good recipe into a venture that earned him fame and fortune.

Other success stories may not be so dramatic, but are

nonetheless wonderful cases of people realizing their dreams or working in a way that meets their needs and motivations. Take Margaret's case, for example. She is employed by a temporary help agency, working the hours she wants, the days she wants, and at the positions and companies she wants. She is working because she wants to, when she wants to, and where she wants to. She earns the money she needs to afford the extras, and still has plenty of time for sewing, bridge, and even acting in her local community theater. If that's not a success story, we don't know what is!

Charlie, who works on a commission basis for a travel agency, is a retired association executive who also wanted to work his own hours in a job that would provide him with some income and some challenge. He plans to go on working every day because that's what keeps him energized and feeling great. He is also working part-time as a mystery shopper for a retailer, and may sign on as a host for a cruise line. (They receive free passage and free meals, he tells us.) Sounds successful to us.

Then there's the story of Neda. She is still working for her employer, a health care organization, but is in her third career with the same employer. She held a position in nursing for nearly twenty years, and then moved to a management position. She now coordinates the company's senior association. She works full-time in a job with high visibility and many challenges and demands. She is happy with her work today. She's not sure what challenge she may tackle next. She is considering the Peace Corps.

Each success story is as unique as the individual's goals, lifestyle, and needs. Success is where you choose to find it, with an employer who values your contribution.

The High Costs of Retirement

Colonel Sanders felt strongly about what the older worker could offer and achieve. The following is a portion of a statement he made before a United States Congressional Committee on Aging on May 25, 1977:

We older folks can have a lot to contribute.

Take Benjamin Franklin. He was seventy years old when he was appointed to the committee that wrote the Declaration of Independence, and he got France to recognize the United States when he was seventy-two. Probably his greatest contribution to this country came when he was eighty-one years old. That's when he almost single-handedly got the factions of Congress—there are always factions, aren't there—to compromise on our Constitution, and then he helped get it ratified.

It was a good thing that he hadn't been forced to retire. We might not have had a country or a constitution.

Thomas Jefferson brought about the founding of the University of Virginia when he was seventy-six.

Thomas Alva Edison kept inventing things long after his sixty-fifth birthday. George C. Marshall was sixty-seven when he designed the European Recovery Program, for which he received the Nobel Prize.

Those are dramatic examples.

There are a lot more folks who have contributed in more common ways, and many who continue to contribute. Now it's not that us older folks are smarter than you youngsters, but at least we've had an opportunity to make most of the common mistakes. We've had our quota of disappointments and burned fingers. We've lost some of the fears and insecurities that plagued our youth. And, to the degree that we've learned from these experiences, we've gained some wisdom.

I'm not against retirement for people who want it. But retirement's just not for me. I believe a man will rust out quicker'n he'll wear out. I'm an 1890 model, and I'm planning to work another thirteen years and then become a senior citizen. . . .

We're wasting a lot of brainpower and energy by making people retire. I'd like to see it stopped.[4]

As the Colonel said, the practice of forced retirement is a waste of a lot of brainpower and energy. Along with this high cost to employers, there can also be a high cost of retirement for you personally.

Retirement may actually be unaffordable—both monetarily and psychologically. Let's look first at the monetary aspect. An article in the July/August 1993 issue of *Issues in HR* reported that a recent survey conducted by William M. Mercer, Inc., of corporate executives indicated that by the year 2000 the average sixty-five-year-old salaried employee will not be able to financially afford retirement. Further, those who *will* be able to retire will have to rely more heavily on personal savings than did prior generations of retirees.

Inactivity in retirement is another reason you may not be able to afford retirement. Physical inactivity contributes to poor health and the loss of strength, and can lead to disease and ultimately death. By simply remaining physically active you can actually reverse some of the physical dimensions of aging.

In addition to the fact that you may not be able to afford retirement financially or physically, there is the fact that retirement may not be the best choice for you in terms of mental health and well-being. "Total retirement is a waste of time, a slow mental death and a denial of seniors' many years of valuable experience," said Dorothy V. Popoff in a letter to the editor in the November 1990 *AARP Bulletin*. One company executive said that all the employees of his company who have taken retirement have died within two years. Whether from lack of mental stimulation, being removed from work that is meaningful and challenging, being isolated from friends and professional colleagues, or losing a sense of purpose in life, many individuals do not live beyond their formal job retirement.

Deepak Chopra, M.D., author of *Ageless Body, Timeless Mind*, states that the oldest people alive today are not merely random survivors, but individuals who embody the values of freedom, independence, and adaptability.

You Can Do What You Want to Do

The choice is yours—and you have so many choices to make in unretirement. You can work full-time or part-time, you can stay within your field or strike out on your own, you can volunteer for your favorite charity or work for hard cash. The hardest part of unretirement may be deciding what it is that *you* want to accomplish. Take some time to analyze your choices and determine which is right for your needs, motivations, lifestyle, and energy. This is uncharted territory on the unretirement trail. Develop your own road map and get started on this great adventure!

The new road to unretirement can be a thrilling one—one in which you can realize your dreams, live up to your potential, embrace life, have fun, and make a difference. Are you ready to begin?

Notes

1. James F. Fries, M.D., *Aging Well* (Reading, Mass.: Addison-Wesley, 1989).
2. Jeffrey G. Allen and Jess Gorkin, *Finding the Right Job at Midlife* (New York: Simon & Schuster, 1985).
3. "AARP Andrus Foundation Report," *Working Age*, July/August 1992, p. 2.
4. Catherine D. Fyock, *America's Work Force Is Coming of Age* (Lexington Books/Macmillan, 1990), pp. 215–217.

Appendix

Resources to Assist You

State Units on Aging
Listed Alphabetically by State

Oscar D. Tucker
Commission on Aging
770 Washington Avenue #470
Montgomery, AL 36130
(205) 242-5743

Constance Sipe
Older Alaskans Commission
PO Box 110209
Juneau, AK 99811–0209
(907) 465-3250

Richard Littler
Aging and Adult
   Administration
1789 West Jefferson, 2SW, 950A
Phoenix, AZ 85007
(602) 542-4446

Herb Sanderson
Division of Aging and Adult
   Services
PO Box 1437
Little Rock, AR 72203–1437
(501) 682-2441

Robert P. Martinez
California Department of
   Aging
1600 K Street
Sacramento, CA 95814
(916) 322-5290

Rita Barreras
Aging and Adult Service
1575 Sherman Street, 4th Floor
Denver, CO 80203–1714
(303) 866-3851

Mary Ellen Klinck
Department on Aging
175 Main Street
Hartford, CT 06106
(203) 566-3238

Eleanor Cain
Division of Aging
1901 North DuPont Highway
New Castle, DE 19720
(302) 577-4791

Veronica Pace
Office on Aging
1424 K Street NW, 2nd Floor
Washington, DC 20005
(202) 724-5626

Rob Lombardo
Program Office for Aging and
   Adult Services
1317 Winewood Boulevard
Tallahassee, FL 32301
(904) 488-8922

Fred McGinnis
Division of Aging Services
Two Peachtree Street,
    18th Floor
Atlanta, GA 30303
(404) 657-5258

D. Renee Anderson
Division of Senior Citizens
PO Box 2816
Agana, Guam 96910

Jeanette Takamura
Executive Office on Aging
335 Merchant Street, Room 241
Honolulu, HI 96813
(808) 548-2593

Charlene Martindale
Office on Aging
Statehouse, Room 108
Boise, ID 83720
(208) 334-3833

Maralee Lindley
Illinois Department on Aging
421 East Capitol Avenue
Springfield, IL 62701
(217) 785-2870

Geneva Shedd
Bureau of Aging
PO Box 7083
Indianapolis, IN 46207–7083
(317) 232-7020

Betty Grandquist
Department of Elder Affairs
914 Grand Avenue
Des Moines, IA 50319
(515) 281-5187

Joanne E. Hurst
Department on Aging
915 SW Harrison
Topeka, KS 66612–1500
(913) 296-4986

Sue Tuttle
Division of Aging Services
275 East Main Street, 5 West
Frankfort, KY 40621
(502) 564-6930

Vickey Hunt
Office of Elderly Affairs
PO Box 80374
Baton Rouge, LA 70898–0374
(504) 925-1700

Christine Gianopoulos
Bureau of Elder and Adult
    Services
State House Station, #11
Augusta, ME 04333
(207) 624-5335

Rosalie Abrams
Office on Aging
301 West Preston Street, Room
    1004
Baltimore, MD 21201
(410) 225-1100

Paul Lanzikos
Executive Office of Elder
    Affairs
One Ashburton Place, #51–LR
Boston, MA 02108–1518
(617) 727-7750

Diane Braunstein
Office of Services to the Aging
PO Box 30026
Lansing, MI 48909
(517) 373-8230

Gerald Bloedow
Board on Aging
444 Lafayette Road, 4th Floor
St. Paul, MN 55155–3843
(612) 296-2770 or (800) 882-6262

Eddie Anderson
Division of Aging and Adult
  Services
455 North Lamar Street
Jackson, MS 39202
(601) 359-6770

Donald Howard
Division on Aging
PO Box 1337
Jefferson City, MO 65102
(314) 751-3082

Eugene Huntington
Department of Family Services
PO Box 8005
Helena, MT 59604
(406) 444-5900

Betsy Palmer
Department on Aging
PO Box 95044
Lincoln, NE 68509
(402) 471-2306

Suzanne Ernst
Division for Aging Services
340 North 11th Street
Las Vegas, NV 89101
(702) 486-3545

Richard Chevrefils
Division of Elderly and Adult
  Services
115 Pleasant Street
Concord, NH 03301–3843
(603) 271-4680

Ann Zahora
Division on Aging
South Broad and Front Streets,
  CN807
Trenton, NJ 08625–0807
(609) 292-4833

Stephanie FallCreek
State Agency on Aging
224 East Palace Ave,
  Ground Floor
Santa Fe, NM 87501
(505) 827-7640

Jane Gould
New York State Office for the
  Aging
Empire State Plaza,
  Building #2
Albany, NY 12223–0001
(518) 474-4425

Bonnie M. Cramer
Division of Aging
Caller Box 29531
Raleigh, NC 27626–0531
(919) 733-3983

Larry Brewster
Aging Services Division
State Capitol Building
Bismarck, ND 58505
(701) 224-2577

Judith Brachman
Department of Aging
50 West Broad Street, 9th Floor
Columbus, OH 43266–0501
(614) 466-5500

Roy Keen
Aging Services Division
PO Box 25352
Oklahoma City, OK 73125
(405) 521-2327

James C. Wilson
Senior Services Division
500 Summer Street NE,
  2nd Floor
Salem, OR 97310–1015
(503) 945-5811

Linda Rhodes
Department of Aging
231 State Street
Harrisburg, PA 17101–1195
(717) 783-1828

Ruby Rodriguez
Office for Elderly Affairs
PO Box 50063, Old San Juan
  Station
San Juan, PR 00902
(809) 721-5710

Maureen Maigret
Department of Elderly Affairs
160 Pine Street
Providence, RI 02903–3708
(401) 277-2858

Ruth Seigler
Governors Office, Division on
  Aging
202 Arbor Lake Drive, Suite 301
Columbia, SC 29223
(803) 737-7500

Gail Ferris
Office of Adult Services for the
  Aging
700 Governors Drive
Pierre, SD 57501
(605) 773-3656

Emily Wiseman
Commission on Aging
706 Church Street, Suite 201
Nashville, TN 37243–0860
(615) 741-2056

O. P. (Bob) Bobbitt
Department of Aging
PO Box 12786 Capitol Station
Austin, TX 78741–3702
(512) 444-2727

Percy Devine III
Division of Aging and Adult
  Services
Box 45500
Salt Lake City, UT 84145–0500
(801) 538-3910

Joel Cook
Department of Aging and
  Disabilities
103 South Main Street
Waterbury, VT 05676
(802) 241-2400

Thelma Bland
Department for the Aging
700 East Franklin Street
Richmond, VA 23219–2327
(804) 225-2271

Bernice Hall
Senior Citizen Affairs
#19 Estate Diamond
  Frederiksted
St. Croix, VI 00840
(809) 772-4950, Ext. 46

Charles Reed
Aging and Adult Services
  Administration
PO Box 45050
Olympia, WA 98504–5050
(206) 586-3768

David Brown
Commission on Aging
Holly Grove, State Capitol
Charleston, WV 25305
(304) 558-3317

Donna McDowell
Bureau on Aging
217 South Hamilton Street,
    Suite 300
Madison, WI 53703
(608) 266-2536

Morris Gardner
Division on Aging
Hathaway Building, Room 139
Cheyenne, WY 82002–0480
(307) 777-7986

Job Training Partnership Offices
Listed Alphabetically by State

Contact these offices to identify local employment and training programs.

Sharon Williams
Eastern Arkansas Private
    Industry Council
600 West Broadway
West Memphis, AR 72303
(501) 735-6730

Martha Jacoby
Western Job Training
    Partnership Association
1100 K Street, Suite 101
Sacramento, CA 95814
(916) 327-7549

Kenneth Nickerson
Job Training Partnership
    Association
1801 16th Street
Greeley, CO 80631
(303) 350-6802

Alex Johnson
Connecticut Job Training
    Association
376 Hartford Turnpike
North Windham, CT 06256
(203) 455-0707

Steve Berman
New England Training and
    Employment Council
140 Huyshope Avenue
Hartford, CT 06106
(203) 525-2099

Maxine Carpenter
Association for Providers of
    Employment and Training
1120 20th Street NW, Suite 200
Washington, DC 20036
(202) 785-1963

Jude Ann Burk
Florida Employment and
    Training Association
1330 Thomasville Road
Tallahassee, FL 32303
(904) 561-8838

Wynn Montgomery
Private Industry Council of
    Atlanta, Inc.
100 Edgewood Avenue,
    Suite 1600
Atlanta, GA 30303

Karen Crawford-Springer
Illinois Employment Training
  Association
100 North First Street,
  Room E432
Springfield, IL 62777
(217) 782-4862

J. D. Murphy
Private Industry Council, Inc.
PO Box 696
Harrisburg, IL 62946

Joyce Duvall
Indiana Job Training
  Administrators
17 West Market, Suite 730
Indianapolis, IN 46204
(317) 684-2359

Pam Van Ast
Economic Developers
2006 South Ankeny Boulevard
Ankeny, IA 50021
(515) 964-6567

Jerry Smith
JTPA Directors Association
209 North Elm
Creston, IA 50801
(515) 782-8591

Sheila Clark
Bluegrass State Association of
  Job Training
300 Hammond Drive
Hopkinsville, KY 42240
(502) 886-9484

Cheryl Lynn
Louisiana SDA Directors
  Association
3501 Fifth Avenue, Suite C–5
Lake Charles, LA 70605
(504) 873-6855

Maryland Institute for
  Employment Training
7201 Rossville Boulevard
Baltimore, MD 21237
(301) 522-5941

Judy Selesnick
Job Training Partnership
  Association of Massachusetts
20 Wheeler Street, 4th Floor
Lynn, MA 01902
(617) 595-0484

Leanne Waite
Michigan Works!
1760 East Grand River,
  Suite 200
East Lansing, MI 48823
(517) 336-7700

Bob Douglas
Missouri Private Industry
  Council Chairs
309 North Jefferson
Saint James, MO 65559

Brenda Gardner
Missouri Training Institute
University of Missouri,
  11 Middlebush Hall
Columbia, MO 65211
(314) 882-2860

Marvin Freeman
Training and Employment
  Administration of Missouri
2115 Parkway Drive
Saint Charles, MO 63301
(314) 441-1577

Jean Koszulinski
Garden State Employment and
  Training Association
Administration Building,
  4th Floor
Elizabeth, NJ 07207
(210) 524-1121

Dee Rosebrock
State Employment and Training
  Commission
CN 940
Trenton, NJ 08625
(609) 292-2490

Eliza Castellano
JTPA Training Section
PO Box 4218
Santa Fe, NM 87502
(505) 827-6850

John Twomey
New York State Association of
  Training and Employment
150 State Street
Albany, NY 12207
(518) 465-1473

Bill Ragland
North Carolina Association of
  Private Industry Councils
36 West Main Street
Brevard, NC 28712
(704) 883-2600

Linda Pappas
North Carolina Employment
  and Training Association
PO Box 2346
Rocky Mount, NC 27802–2346
(919) 442-4532

David Turrentine
North Carolina Job Training
  Administration Association
PO Box 1717
New Bern, NC 28560
(919) 638-3185

Carol Wargo
Ohio Management Training
  Institute
2700 East Dublin Granville
  Road
Columbus, OH 43229
(614) 895-7500

Phylis Frazer
Ohio Manpower Association
150 Fair Street
Hillsboro, OH 45133
(513) 393-1933

Janet Noakes
Oregon Employment and
  Training Association
3217 Northeast 33rd
Portland, OR 97212
(503) 282-1706

Virginia Joyce
Pennsylvania Service Delivery
  Area Association
121 State Street, 2nd Floor
Harrisburg, PA 17101
(717) 234-5627

Anne McCafferty
The Pittsburgh Partnership
404 City-County Building
Pittsburgh, PA 15219
(412) 255-2696

John Baker
Texas Association of Private
    Industry Councils
815 Brazos, Suite 802
Austin, TX 78701
(512) 477-7787

Sidney Jefferies
Private Industry Council, Inc.
2510 Washington Boulevard,
    Suite 238
Ogden, UT 84401
(801) 399-8850

Rosalyn Icey
Virginia Association of Service
    Delivery Areas
5410 Williamsburg Road
Sandston, VA 23150
(804) 226-1941

Elaine Maull
Southwest Washington Private
    Industry Council
1950 Fort Vancouver Way,
    Suite B
Vancouver, WA 98663
(206) 696-8417

Earl Davenport
Washington Private Industry
    Council Association
Route 1 Box 43
Colville, WA 99114
(509) 684-8750

Dale Hopkins
Department of Industry, Labor,
    and Human Relations
PO Box 7972
Madison, WI 53707–7972
(608) 266-0327

Displaced Homemaker Network
Listed Alphabetically by State

Contact these offices for information on displaced homemaker
employment programs.

Displaced Homemakers
    Program
2601 Carson Road
Birmingham, AL 35215
(205) 867-4832

Alaska Women's Resource
    Center
111 West Ninth Avenue
Anchorage, AK 99501
(907) 276-0528

Center for New Directions
1430 North Second Street
Phoenix, AZ 85004
(602) 252-0918

Choices: Career Development
    Center
103 West Park
Bald Knob, AR 72010
(501) 724-6306

Turning Point Career Center,
    YWCA
2600 Bancroft Way
Berkeley, CA 94704
(415) 848-6370

Empowerment Program
1245 East Colfax Avenue, #404
Denver, CO 80218
(303) 863-7817

Displaced Homemakers
  Program, YWCA
753 Fairfield Avenue
Bridgeport, CT 06604
(203) 334-6154

Women's Vocational Services
Route 113, Box 548
Georgetown, DE 19947
(302) 856-5325

Wider Opportunities for
  Women
1325 G Street NW, LL
Washington, DC 20005
(202) 638-3143

Women in Transition
1519 Clearlake Road
Cocoa, FL 32922
(407) 632-1111, Ext. 4600

Single Parent/Displaced
  Homemaker Program
Route 12, Box 1273
Valdosta, GA 31602
(912) 333-2100

Single Parent/Displaced
  Homemaker Program
4303 Diamond Head Road,
  Ilima 103
Honolulu, HI 96816
(808) 734-9500

Career Center, YWCA
720 West Washington Street
Boise, ID 83702
(208) 336-7306

Women Employed Institute
22 West Monroe, Suite 1400
Chicago, IL 60603
(312) 782-3902

South Central Workforce
  Development Services
PO Box 1266
Bloomington, IN 47402
(812) 332-3777

Displaced Homemakers
  Program
Box 400
Calmar, IA 52132
(319) 562-3263

Single Parent/Displaced
  Homemaker Program
125 South Second
Arkansas City, KS 67005
(316) 442-0430

Creative Employment Project
226 West Breckinridge Street
Louisville, KY 40203
(502) 581-7237

Center for Displaced
  Homemakers
7393 Florida Boulevard
Baton Rouge, LA 70806
(504) 925-6922

Displaced Homemakers
  Program
Stoddard House, University of
  Maine
Augusta, ME 04330–9410
(207) 621-3440

Displaced Homemaker
  Program, YWCA
167 Duke of Gloucester Street
Annapolis, MD 21401
(301) 269-0378

Women's Job Counseling
   Center
34 Follen Street
Cambridge, MA 01238
(617) 864-9097

Displaced Homemaker
   Program
PO Box 797
Alpena, MI 49707
(517) 356-6569

Working Opportunities for
   Women, New Careers
2700 University Avenue, #120
St. Paul, MN 55114
(612) 647-9961

Single Parent/Displaced
   Homemakers Program
487 North Union Extension
Canton, MS 39046
(601) 859-3925

Displaced Homemakers
   Program
2601 NE Barry Road
Kansas City, MO 64156
(816) 437-3095

Displaced Homemakers
   Program, YWCA
909 Wyoming Avenue
Billings, MT 59101
(406) 245-6879

Displaced Homemakers
   Program, YWCA
234 East Third
Grand Island, NE 68801
(308) 384-8170

Single Parent/Displaced
   Homemaker Program
2201 West Nye Lane
Carson City, NV 89703
(702) 887-3000

Assisting People in Transition
2020 Riverside Drive
Berlin, NH 03584
(603) 752-1113

Displaced Homemaker
   Program
523 Lake Avenue
Asbury Park, NJ 07712
(908) 776-2668

Displaced Homemakers
   Program
4001 Indian School Road NE,
   #220
Albuquerque, NM 87110
(505) 841-4662

New York Women's
   Employment Center
198 Broadway, Suite 200
New York, NY 10038
(212) 964-8934

Wider Opportunities for
   Women
PO Box 35009
Charlotte, NC 28235
(704) 342-6532

Single Parent/Displaced
   Homemakers Program
214 West Bowen
Bismarck, ND 58504
(701) 221-3791

Displaced Homemaker
  Program
147 Park Street
Akron, OH 44308
(216) 253-5142

Displaced Homemakers
  Program
1121 North Spurgeon
Altus, OK 73521
(405) 477-2439

Turning Point Transitions
Linn-Benton Community
  College
6500 Pacific Boulevard SW
Albany, OR 97321
(503) 967-6112

New Choices
Altoona Area Vo-Tech School
1500 Fourth Avenue
Altoona, PA 16602
(814) 946-8454

Single Parent Program
70 Metropolitan Avenue
Cranston, RI 02920
(401) 785-0400

Single Parent/Displaced
  Homemaker Program
165 St. Philip Street (PO Box
  22132)
Charleston, SC 29413
(803) 723-7138

Senior Worker Program
421 South Main
Aberdeen, SD 57401
(605) 622-2298

Employment and Training
  Program, YWCA
1608 Woodmont Boulevard
Nashville, TN 37215
(615) 269-9922

Displaced Homemakers
  Program
Amarillo College
PO Box 447
Amarillo, TX 79178
(806) 371-5450

Davis Applied Technology
  Center
Displaced Homemaker
  Program
550 East 300 South
Kaysville, UT 84037
(801) 546-4134

Displaced Homemaker
  Program
PO Drawer 1127
Dublin, VA 24084
(703) 674-3600, Ext. 427

Women's Programs, Grays
  Harbor College
1620 Edward P. Smith Drive
Aberdeen, WA 98520
(206) 532-9020

Center for Economic Options
601 Delaware Avenue
Charleston, WV 25302
(304) 345-1298

Starting Point
PO Box 2277
Appleton, WI 54913–2277
(414) 735-5710

YWCA Transitional Services
PO Box 1667
Rock Springs, WY 82902
(307) 362-7923

Organizations and Services for Older Americans

AARP
601 E Street NW
Washington, DC 20049
(202) 434-2277

ACTION, Older American
   Programs
1100 Vermont Avenue NW, 6th
   Floor
Washington, DC 20525
(202) 606-4855

Administration on Aging
330 Independence Avenue SW
Washington, DC 20201
(202) 619-0641

Aging in America
1500 Pelham Parkway
Bronx, NY 10461
(718) 824-4004

Alliance for Aging Research
2021 K Street NW, #305
Washington, DC 20006
(202) 293-2856

American Foundation for the
   Blind
15 West 16th Street
New York, NY 10011
(212) 620-2000

American Red Cross
Public Inquiry Center
18th and D Streets NW
Washington, DC 20006
(202) 639-3233

American Society on Aging
833 Market Street, Suite 512
San Francisco, CA 94103
(415) 882-2910

Association for Adult
   Development and Aging
5999 Stevenson Avenue
Alexandria, VA 22304
(703) 823-9800

Center for the Study of Aging
706 Madison Avenue
Albany, NY 12208-3695
(518) 465-6927

Center for Understanding
   Aging
PO Box 246
Southington, CT 06489–0246
(203) 621-2079

Consumer Information Catalog
Pueblo, CO 81009
(719) 948-4000

Department of Labor
Consumer Affairs, Room S1032
200 Constitution Avenue NW
Washington, DC 20210
(202) 219-6060

Disabled American Veterans
807 Maine Avenue SW
Washington, DC 20024
(202) 554-3501

Elderhostel
75 Federal Street
Boston, MA 02110–1941
(617) 426-7788

Elvirita Lewis Foundation
PO Box 1539
La Quinta, CA 92253
(619) 564-1780

Equal Employment
  Opportunity Commission
1801 L Street NW
Washington, DC 20507
(800) 663-4900

Federal Council on the Aging
330 Independence SW, Room
  4280 HHS–N
Washington, DC 20201
(202) 619-2451

Gray Panthers
2025 Pennsylvania Avenue NW,
  #821
Washington, DC 20006
(202) 387-3111

Green Thumb, Inc.
2000 North 14th Street,
  Suite 800
Arlington, VA 22201
(703) 522-7272

Institute on Aging
Columbia University
622 West 113th Street
New York, NY 10025
(212) 854-2513

Legal Services for the Elderly
130 West 42nd Street,
  17th Floor
New York, NY 10036
(212) 391-0120

National Alliance of Senior
  Citizens
1700 18th Street NW, Suite 401
Washington, DC 20009
(202) 986-0117

National Asian Pacific Center
  on Aging
1511 Third Avenue, #914
Seattle, WA 98101
(206) 624-1221

National Association for
  Hispanic Elderly
3325 Wilshire Boulevard, Suite
  800
Los Angeles, CA 90010–1724
(213) 487-1922

National Association for
  Human Development
1424 16th Street NW, Suite 102
Washington, DC 20036
(202) 328-2191

National Association of Area
  Agencies on Aging
1112 16th Street NW, Suite 100
Washington, DC 20036
(202) 296-8130

National Association of Meal
  Programs
204 E Street NE
Washington, DC 20002
(202) 547-6157

National Association of State
  Units on Aging
1225 I Street NW, Suite 725
Washington, DC 20005
(202) 898-2578

National Caucus and Center on
  Black Aged
1424 K Street NW, Suite 500
Washington, DC 20005
(202) 637-8400

National Commission on
  Working Women
1325 G Street NW, Lower Level
Washington, DC 20005
(202) 638-3143

National Committee for
  Employment Policy
1522 K Street NW, Suite 300
Washington, DC 20005

National Council of Senior
  Citizens
1331 F Street NW
Washington, DC 20004–1171
(202) 347-8800

National Council on the Aging
409 Third Street SW, Suite 200
Washington, DC 20024
(202) 479-1200

National Displaced
  Homemakers Network
1625 K Street, Suite 300
Washington, DC 20006
(202) 467-6346

National Indian Council on
  Aging
6400 Uptown Boulevard NE,
  #510–W
Albuquerque, NM 87110
(505) 888-3302

National Self-Help
  Clearinghouse
25 West 43rd St., Room 620
New York, NY 10036
(212) 642-2944

National Senior Citizens Law
  Center
1815 H Street NW, Suite 700
Washington, DC 20006
(202) 887-5280

National Urban League
500 East 62nd Street
New York, NY 10021
(212) 310-9210

Older Women's League
666 11th Street NW, #700
Washington, DC 20001
(202) 783-6686

Organization of Chinese
  Americans
1001 Connecticut Avenue NW,
  Room 707
Washington, DC 20036
(202) 223-5500

Social Security Administration
6401 Security Boulevard
Baltimore, MD 21235
(800) 234-5772

Special Committee on Aging
Room G-31, DSOB
Washington, DC 20510

United States Department of
  Labor
Division of Older Worker
  Programs
200 Constitution Avenue NW,
  #N–4641
Washington, DC 20210
(202) 535-0521

United States Senate
Special Committee on Aging
Room G-31, DSOB
Washington, DC 20510

Wider Opportunities for
  Women
1325 G Street NW, Lower Level
Washington, DC 20005
(202) 638-3143

Suggested Reading

Anthony, Rebecca Jespersen, and Gerald Roe. *Over 40 and Looking for Work? A Guide for the Unemployed, Underemployed, and Unhappily Employed*. Holbrook, Mass.: Bob Adams, Inc., 1991.

Azrin, Nathan H., and Victoria Besalel. *Finding a Job*. Berkeley, Calif.: Ten Speed Press, 1983.

Bird, Caroline. *Second Careers: New Ways to Work after 50*. New York: Little, Brown, and Company, 1992.

Birsner, E. Patricia. *Mid-Career Job Hunting: Official Handbook of the Forty-Plus Club*. New York: Simon & Schuster/ARCO, 1991.

Bolles, Richard N. *The Three Boxes of Life and How to Get Out of Them*. Berkeley, Calif.: Ten Speed Press, 1981.

———. *What Color Is Your Parachute? A Practical Manual for Job Hunters and Career Changers*. Berkeley, Calif.: Ten Speed Press, 1993.

Brontë, Lydia. *The Longevity Factor: The New Reality of Long Careers and How It Can Lead to Richer Lives*. New York: Harper Collins, 1993.

Cohen, Herb. *You Can Negotiate Anything*. Secaucus, N.J.: Citadel Press, 1983.

Connor, J. Robert. *Cracking the Over-50 Job Market*. New York: Penguin Books, 1992.

Crystal, John, and Richard Bolles. *Where Do I Go From Here With My Life?* Berkeley, Calif.: Ten Speed Press, 1974.

Dychtwald, Ken, and Joe Flower. *Age Wave*. Los Angeles: Tarcher, Inc., 1989.

Figler, Howard. *The Complete Job-Search Handbook: All the Skill You Need to Get Any Job and Have a Good Time Doing It*. New York: Henry Holt and Company, 1988.

Fyock, Catherine D. *America's Work Force Is Coming of Age: What Every Business Needs to Know to Recruit, Train, Manage, and Retain an Aging Work Force*. Lexington, Mass.: Lexington Books/Macmillan, 1990.

Hansen, Katharine. *Dynamic Cover Letters*. Berkeley, Calif.: Ten Speed Press, 1990.

Jackson, Tom. *The Perfect Résumé*. New York: Bantam Books, 1990.

Kanchier, Carole. *Dare to Change Your Job—and Your Life*. New York: Mastermedia Limited, 1991.

Krannich, Caryl Rae, and Ronald L. Krannich. *The Best Jobs for the 1990s and Into the 21st Century.* Woodbridge, Va.: Impact Publications, 1991.

———. *Careering and Re-Careering for the 1990s.* Woodbridge, Va.: Impact Publications, 1991.

———. *Dynamite Answers to Interview Questions.* Woodbridge, Va.: Impact Publications, 1991.

———. *Network Your Way to Job and Career Success,* Woodbridge, Va.: Impact Publications, 1989.

Lathrop, Richard. *Who's Hiring Who? How to Find That Job Fast!* Berkeley, Calif.: Ten Speed Press, 1989.

Mackay, Harvey. *Swim With the Sharks Without Being Eaten Alive.* New York: Ballantine Books, 1988.

Marsh, Deloss. *Retirement Careers: Combining the Best of Work and Leisure.* Charlotte, Vt.: Williamson Publishing, 1991.

McGinnis, Alan Loy. *The Power of Optimism.* New York: Harper & Row, 1990.

Medley, H. Anthony. *Sweaty Palms: The Neglected Art of Being Interviewed.* Berkeley, Calif.: Ten Speed Press, 1992.

Merman, Stephen K., and John E. McLaughlin. *Out-Interviewing the Interviewer: A Job Winner's Script for Success.* Englewood Cliffs, N.J.: Prentice-Hall, 1983.

Morgan, John S. *Getting a Job After 50.* Princeton, N.J.: Petrocelli Books, 1987.

Parker, Yana. *The Damn Good Résumé Guide.* Berkeley, Calif.: Ten Speed Press, 1989.

Peale, Norman Vincent. *The Power of Positive Thinking.* Englewood Cliffs, N.J.: Prentice-Hall, 1952.

Petras, Kathryn, and Ross Petras. *The Over-40 Job Guide.* New York: Simon & Schuster/Poseidon, 1993.

Pettus, Theodore. *One on One: Win the Interview, Win the Job.* New York: Random House, 1981.

Ray, Samuel N. *Job Hunting After 50.* New York: John Wiley and Sons, 1991.

———. *Résumés for the Over-50 Job Hunter.* New York: John Wiley and Sons, 1993.

Sacharov, Al. *Offbeat Careers.* Berkeley, Calif.: Ten Speed Press, 1988.

Sher, Barbara, with Annie Gottlieb. *Wishcraft: How to Get What You Really Want*. New York: Ballantine Books, 1979.

Sinetar, Marsha. *Do What You Love, the Money Will Follow*. New York: Dell Publishing, 1987.

Social Security Administration. *How Work Affects Your Social Security Checks*. Washington, D.C.: Social Security Administration, 1992.

Wells, Joel. *Who Do You Think You Are?* Chicago: Thomas More Press, 1989.

Whitmyer, Claude, Salli Rasberry, and Michael Phillips. *Running a One-Person Business*. Berkeley, Calif.: Ten Speed Press, 1989.

Yate, Martin. *Cover Letters That Knock 'em Dead*. Holbrook, Mass.: Bob Adams, Inc., 1992.

———. *Knock 'em Dead: The Ultimate Job Seeker's Handbook*. Holbrook, Mass.: Bob Adams, Inc., 1993.

———. *Knock 'em Dead With Great Answers to Tough Interview Questions*. Holbrook, Mass.: Bob Adams, Inc., 1988.

———. *Résumés That Knock 'em Dead*. Holbrook, Mass.: Bob Adams, Inc., 1992.

Index

abilities assessment, 95–96
absenteeism, reduced, 14, 19, 33–34
accident-proneness, of un-retirees, 36–37
action strategies, 57–60
  for retraining, 144–145
  for staying active in field, 71–72
action verbs, 77, 78–79
Aerospace Corp., casual employ-ment program of, 66–67
age discrimination, 4–5, 71, 123–135
  fighting back against, 18
  rise in claims of, 14–15
Age Discrimination in Employ-ment Act (ADEA), 7, 123, 124, 129–130
ageism, 71, 123, 125, 129–135
Ageless Body, Timeless Mind (Chopra), 157
"The Age of Indifference," 12
Age Wave (Dychtwald), 135
aging, 6, 152–153
  slowing down of, 150–151
  state units on, 159–163
Aging Well (Fries), 150
Allen, Jeffrey G., on positive talk, 151–152

American Association of Retired Persons (AARP)
  Talent Bank of, 59
  training study by, 138
  Worker Equity report by, 8
Americans with Disabilities Act (ADA), 113, 123–125
America's Work Force Is Coming of Age (Fyock), 4–5
application form, 111–114
aptitude tests, 86
Armed Services Vocational Aptitude Battery, 86
association, law of, 140
attitudinal barriers, 147–150
Axel, Helen, on networking, 89

baby boomers, 5, 11, 13–14
baby busters, 11–12
barriers, 20–21, 71
  attitudinal, 147–150
Be an Outrageous Older Woman (Jacobs), 152–153
Bilhartz, John, counseling ser-vice of, 83–86
Bird, Caroline, older worker survey by, 10, 20
Blueprint for Success (Myers), 49
Bolles, Richard, on job options for unretirees, 62–64